Instant
EXPERT

Tradition » Passion » Perfection

Linda O'Keeffe is a journalist and fashion expert who has contributed to *Cosmopolitan, Harper's Bazaar, GQ, Details, New York Times Magazine, ELLE*, and numerous other publications. She also lectures on fashion and design, and appears regularly on radio and television. She has written several books, including *Shoes*, which chronicles the history of women's footwear. Originally from Britain, she now lives with an eclectic collection of shoes in New York City.

Princeton Architectural Press
37 East Seventh Street
New York, NY 10003
Visit our website at www.papress.com

Conceived and produced by
Elwin Street Productions
3 Percy Street
London W1T 1DE
www.elwinstreet.com

Illustrations: Tonwen Jones

Picture credits: James Berglie: p. 97; Emma Blau: p. 117;
Corbis: p. 35; Cati Gonzalez: p. 15; Getty: pp. 19, 89; Julia
Galdo: p. 27; Aranka Isani: p. 49; Noah Kalina: p. 39;
Michael McGarry: p. 73; iStockphoto: p. 59.

ISBN: 978-1-61689-222-7
Library of Congress Cataloguing-in-Publication Data is
available from the publisher upon request

SHOES

Linda O'Keeffe

Princeton Architectural Press, New York

Contents

Why be an expert about shoes?

Shoes are much more than mere fashion accessories. On the one hand they are eminently utilitarian. They protect us from the elements, stabilize our bodies, and regulate our gait. But while they serviceably ground and support us, they also caress our feet, elevate our spirits, and feed our fantasies. The relationship we have with our shoes is more often a passion for possession than practicality.

A true shoe aficionado is invariably on a quest when she shops. She has personally experienced the physiological and emotional transformations brought on by an exquisitely designed pair of heels, so her primary motivation tends to be acquisition rather than need and she'll invariably find displeasure in an inferior pair of shoes. She's vigilant about quality because she knows that a toecap detail, heel height, or sole color reveals far more than her character and touches on her psyche.

A larger-than-average shoe collection allows us to express the full spectrum of our personalities, from tomboy to seductress. Shoes can sometimes even be seen as tokens of salvation—the potency of a red shoe or a particular shape of boot is corroborated by an endless number of fairy tales, myths, wedding rituals, folklore, and superstitions.

We're also wise enough never to give up on a pair of shoes we haven't worn in years because we know fashion to be cyclical, which means that today's passé style will evolve into tomorrow's "must have." Most of us see shoes as unconditional mood elevators akin to non-fattening chocolate or as true friends who, unlike our favorite dress or skirt, won't reject us when we gain a few pounds. In fact, as devout shoe fans, our main regret is that we can't wear more than one pair of our favorites at a time.

This passion for shoes is justified when considering the skill, creativity, and craftsmanship that go into their production—the art of shoemaking makes these essentially utilitarian items worthy of our enthusiasm and desire. The ancient skill of cobbling converts formless materials into a beautifully proportioned piece of architecture that acts as a second skin and strikes some as pure alchemy. Nowadays most shoes are mass-produced by machines and computers, so shoes that show signs of handcrafting are deservedly prized and coveted.

Footwear created by the hands of master designers like Manolo Blahnik and Christian Louboutin are tools of seduction that showcase erotic zones. After all, feet have waists, toes have décolletage, and heeled shoes have breasts and throats. Casual shoes require reliable materials and designers with well-regarded reputations because we rely on them to take us through long periods when we tax our bodies. Comfort shoes are essential wardrobe components for anyone with problem feet.

For most of history shoes were marginal, hidden away under long garments and trailing hems, but nowadays they've come into their own and occupy center stage. A classic fashion rule states categorically that shoes should never upstage an outfit but this falls down in the case of an ensemble comprised of generic jeans and a T-shirt. That's when shoes—whether Ferragamos, Timberlands, Uggs, or Doc Martens; whether they derive their beauty from exquisite materials, sexy contours, serviceability, or supreme comfort—actually become the outfit.

The shoes and designers featured in these pages capture our passion for shoes. You'll find a selection of handmade and bespoke shoemakers, a range of some of the most renowned and accomplished luxury designers, as well as those whose focus is on comfort and everyday wear. A few brands of particular note have been highlighted as "Expert Essentials." You'll also find useful information regarding styles, measurements, and maintenance to make sure you get the best out of your collection of shoes and help fuel your fervor for this most coveted and adored of fashion items.

» Fundamentals

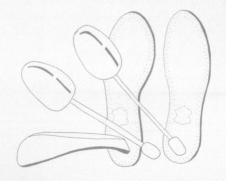

Shoe styles

All styles of women's footwear originally derived from men's styles. Clogs, sandals, moccasins, riding and cowboy boots have always been unisex styles to an extent, but in the last few decades there have been more uniquely female style variations than during all the earlier centuries put together.

The choice of different styles available in women's shoes can be quite breathtaking, and occasionally confusing, so it helps to have a quick reference guide to get them all clear in your mind. The following is a collection of the most common styles that you are likely to encounter, detailing the particular features that characterize each one.

Ballerina: A flat, low-cut leather or cloth pump with a closed toe and slipper-style construction.

Boot: Any enclosed footwear that extends to the ankle, calf, or over the knee.

Clog: A shoe or sandal that's entirely made of wood, or wooden-soled with a cloth or leather upper.

D'Orsay: A heeled dress pump with V shapes cut into the sides of its upper to expose the arch of the foot.

Earth shoe: The generic term for an open, flat sandal where the footbed parallels the contours of the anatomical sole.

D'Orsay heel

Espadrille: A shoe or sandal with a flexible sole that's covered in rope or hemp.

High top: A high-cut, lace-up sports shoe or sneaker that ends just above the ankle.

Jelly: Mass-produced, strappy, flat sandals that are injection-molded from PVC.

Oxford

Loafer: A lightweight slip-on with an apron vamp that has either a foldover tongue or an instep strap across its throat.

Mary Jane: A single-strap pump named after a character in the Buster Brown comic strip. Also called a bar shoe.

Moccasin: A soft, flexible, leather shoe or slipper made from a turned construction where the sole and sides are cut from one piece of leather that's attached to its vamp.

Mule: A shoe or slipper with no quarters so its back is open.

Oxford: A laced shoe with eyelet tabs stitched under the vamp. The woman's version is sometimes called a Gibson.

Platform: A solid integrated sole that has no discernible heel.

Plimsoll: A lace-up, canvas, sports shoe with a rubber sole.

Pump or court shoe: A heeled, or flat, enclosed, slip-on shoe without any closures. A pilgrim's pump

Mary Jane

has a decorative buckle attached to its vamp.

Sandal: The most ancient style of footwear, where the sole is held on the foot with straps or ties.

Slide: A backless slip-on shoe with an open toe.

Spectator

Slingback: A shoe that attaches to the foot with a strap or sling that replaces a closed back quarter.

Slipper: A soft-soled indoor slip-on constructed from a decorative, luxurious, or tactile material.

Sneaker: A rubber-soled sports shoe.

Spectator: A shoe with a light-colored upper and contrasting toecap and counter.

Stiletto: A high-heeled pump with a thin, high heel, and often a pointed toe.

Thong: A flat sandal held on the foot by a strap that originates under the first two toes.

Wellington: A calf-length, pull-on boot, based on the leather Hessian boot. It is traditionally made of rubber.

Wellington

Heel types

On top of shoe styles, there are also different types and shapes of heel. You may find certain styles easier or more comfortable to walk in, while others will be more suitable for particular occasions.

Cuban: A straight-sided, low or medium heel with a curvature or gentle taper to its neck.

Kitten: A short, slender heel with a slight curve that is set forward from the edge of the shoe.

Louis: A breasted heel with a reverse curve and a flared base. Also called a "spool," "pompadour," and "hourglass."

Stacked: Variously shaped heels that are built from visible layers of leather or some other material.

Wedge: A heel of any height that extends from the sole to the ground.

Appropriating men's boots

Historically, there were similarities between styles of footwear for working-class men and women, but an educated woman in mannish footwear often spelled sedition. The suffragettes used menswear detailing in their heeled, buttoned boots and by the mid-20th century, the tides had turned and Marlene Dietrich, dressed in a morning suit and Oxfords, was widely revered for her androgynous beauty.

Shoe materials

Adding to the multiditude of footwear options are the different types of materials available:

Bronze leather: Leather traditionally finished with cochineal to give it a semi-iridescent sheen.

Boarded leather: Leather where embossing, stamping, or indenting creates a variety of faux effects and patterns.

Brocade: A woven fabric that incorporates colored or metallic threads.

Calf: Leather made from the hide of a young cow, prized for its softness.

Damask: Linen, silk, or cotton with a flat jacquard woven pattern.

Kid: Leather made from goatskin.

Nubuck: Leather sanded on the grain side to give a velvety surface.

Patent: Leather with a shiny, waterproof plasticized coating.

Snakeskin: Python and other types of snakeskin used to make uppers and trims.

Satin: A smooth silk or rayon fabric woven with a glossy face and a dull back.

Suede: The grain side of leather that has been sanded to raise its nap.

Words from the wise

Diana Broussard, Designer and shoe consultant for fashion houses including Calvin Klein, Dior, and Gucci

» Origins and quality

The difference between shoes made in Italy or France and China can be enormous or subtle. Chinese factories are technically adept at constructing and duplicating patterns, but they don't have Europe's generational heritage of shoe craftsmanship. That means they don't necessarily have a nuanced approach to materials and the myriad of elusive elements that lend flare to a dress shoe. To definitively evaluate whether a shoe came from Asia or Europe it would need to be taken apart so that the quality can be assessed. In a quick appraisal the European shoe tends to be heavier because more thought, and consequently more materials, went into its internal construction to ensure comfort and durability (although Manolos are exquisitely made and as light as a feather). There's also that unmistakably intoxicating smell of quality leather. At the end of the day, if a shoe caresses your foot and you're emotionally attached to it, where it was made is almost immaterial.

Footwear essentials

However many shoes you may own, there are a few basic styles of which every woman should have at least one pair. Shoe closet essentials involve a handful of styles with multiple personalities that can be casual, conservative, cultivated, and carefree at one and the same time. When it comes to pumps and boots, black is the most versatile color although cowboy and hiking boots are just as serviceable in dark brown. On the other hand there are no hard and fast rules when it comes to the color of sandals.

Boots: A stylish pair of low- to high-heeled, dark, day to evening knee-length boots.

Flats: A comfortable pair of ballet slippers or flat pumps, light enough to transport in a handbag and sturdy enough to act as an antidote to a pair of painful high heels.

Pumps: Classic, mid-heel, dark-colored pumps that easily team up with a conservative interview suit and also set off a pair of trousers.

High heels: One pair of fun, special-occassion high heels.

Sneakers: Gym shoes or high-impact sports trainers.

Cowboy or hiking boots: Stylish enough for city wear and functional on a rough terrain.

Sandals: Flat thongs, mules, or mid-heel open-toed shoes.

A well-made shoe

It's important to make sure you can spot a high-quality and well-made shoe, and make sure you're not overpaying for a second-rate product. There are a number of signs to look out for when picking out a shoe to make sure that the pair you buy are of the highest quality.

>> **Knowing the signs**

A full-grain leather shoe is the top of the line (see page 18). Its surface is never overtly shiny (even if it is patent) and its color has depth. You should never find loose threads or glue remnants on a well-made shoe and all of its seams and edges should feel smooth and relatively soft to your bare foot.

There's a direct correlation between a shoe's price and the number of stages that go into its production, so don't necessarily equate a high price with quality when a shoe has multiple seams and sections in its upper and heel. Similarly don't expect a classic, unembellished pump to have a lower price tag.

A pair of good-quality shoes may not be absolutely symmetrical and barely detectable dissimilarities between the left and right shoe may show the traces of the craftsman's hands.

» Full-grain leather

The majority of women's luxury shoes are constructed from cow hide, and from full-grain leather in particular. Prized for its versatility and durability it easily adapts to any shape of foot, continues to breathe in all temperatures and levels of humidity, and with regular conditioning, will keep its good looks for decades. Corrected grain or polished calf is often mistaken for full grain particularly in American shoes, where all qualities are uniformly classified as "leather." Corrected leather refers to the scars, marks, and imperfections in the lowest quality skins that have been sanded and disguised with layers of synthetics. It's often hard to distinguish corrected from full-grain uppers on brand new shoes, although an extra shiny finish is often a giveaway—so if you are a patent shoe lover be particularly vigilant! Corrected leather shoes are often a false economy because once worn they can crease severely, age badly, and under stress their top surface may sometimes literally flake off.

Opposite: A shoemaker sewing a
sole onto a leather shoe.

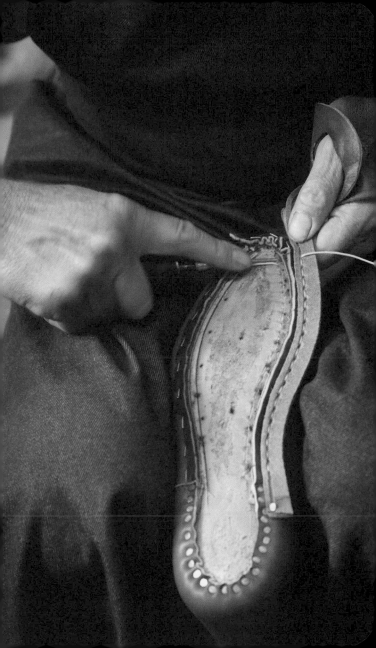

Anatomy of a shoe

Some terms describing the different parts of
the shoe may not be familiar to everyone, but it
is worth understanding what is meant when we
refer to the vamp, for example.

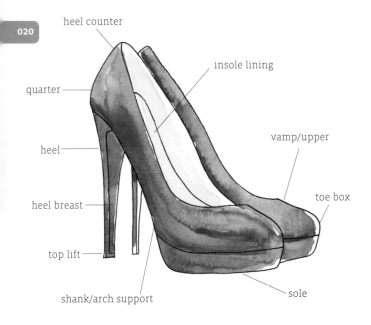

heel counter

insole lining

quarter

vamp/upper

heel

toe box

heel breast

top lift

shank/arch support

sole

Sizes and measurements

The associations between tiny feet and female desirability date back to ancient times, so it comes as no surprise that 88 percent of women regularly choose shoes that are too small for their feet.

Ill-fitting shoes cause a plethora of problems though. When they are too tight they can produce blisters, back, or knee pain. If they are too narrow they can damage nerve tissue and produce tingling, numbness, or benign growths. When they are too wide and the foot is able to slide from side to side they can erode your sense of balance. So it is important to make sure you are wearing shoes that are the correct size.

≫ Measuring systems

A shoe's size refers to its length; most women perceive their size as standardized even though the footwear industry has no universally regulated system of measurement. A person's foot girth also fluctuates with age, weight loss or gain, pregnancy, and prolonged periods of walking in bare feet.

There are a number of shoe-measuring systems and some are based on archaic units like the barleycorn in the UK and USA or the Paris point in continental Europe. A German size may differ from its French equivalent, even though they are both based on the same scale. An international Mondopoint takes foot width into consideration, while the Asian system is metrically based.

When mass production first transformed the clothing industry, shoes customarily came in a variety of incremental A to E widths, but nowadays a shoe's width is at the discretion of each designer and most of them take a "one size fits all" approach. Some particularly coveted lines from maestros like Manolo Blahnik and Christian Louboutin run small and narrow compared to many of their counterparts' designs, which is why shoe aficionados tend to evaluate brands according to whether they are "true to size" (TTS).

Risky heels

Between the 14th and 17th centuries courtesans in Venice liked to venture out in platform shoes called chopines that measured up to 20 inches, a ludicrous fashion that resulted in regular tumbles. Today things seem to have changed little. Supermodel Naomi Campbell shot into notoriety when 10-inch-high moc croc platforms caused her downfall during a 1995 Vivienne Westwood runway show. The super-elevated shoes are currently one of the most popular exhibits in London's Victoria & Albert Museum's Costume Gallery. And there are plenty of images of Lady Gaga on her hands and knees after an ignoble topple wearing Noritaka Tatehana's 10-inch-high gravity-defying platforms.

>> Trying on shoes

It's best to try on new shoes at the end of the day when your feet are fatigued. You'll be more attracted to comfort and less likely to be seduced by style alone. Most of us have one foot that's larger than the other, so gauge your size on your larger foot (it is most often opposite from the hand you write with). Evaluate the fit of both shoes from a standing position with both feet planted firmly and your body weight distributed as evenly as possible, then test walk them around the store. Always try on a half size larger and a half size smaller than the size you think you may need. There's no questioning the value of a knowledgeable salesperson, but only you can truly define and decide on your perfect fit.

>> The ideal fit

In general, a shoe that's too large is more preferable than a shoe that's too tight. Insoles and heel grips are easily inserted and slingback straps can be shortened, but if a shoe is too small nothing can alter its length. Its width can be stretched although that may throw the design out of proportion. Stretching should always be done gradually so never take a cherished shoe to an unfamiliar cobbler. Instead, buy stretchers and begin the process gradually. Advice about breaking in tight high-heeled shoes in a superstore with the aid of a pushcart or expanding shoes by dousing them with rubbing alcohol and molding them to your feet with a hair drier are urban myths rather than solid suggestions.

International shoe sizes

Europe	UK		USA and Canada	
	M	**W**	**M**	**W**
35	3	$2^1/_2$	$3^1/_2$	5
$35^1/_2$	$3^1/_2$	3	4	$5^1/_2$
36	4	$3^1/_2$	$4^1/_2$	6
37	$4^1/_2$	4	5	$6^1/_2$
$37^1/_2$	5	$4^1/_2$	$5^1/_2$	7
38	$5^1/_2$	5	6	$7^1/_2$
$38^1/_2$	6	$5^1/_2$	$6^1/_2$	8
39	$6^1/_2$	6	7	$8^1/_2$
40	7	$6^1/_2$	$7^1/_2$	9
41	$7^1/_2$	7	8	$9^1/_2$
42	8	$7^1/_2$	$8^1/_2$	10
43	$8^1/_2$	8	9	$10^1/_2$
44	10	$9^1/_2$	$10^1/_2$	12
45	11	$10^1/_2$	$11^1/_2$	13
$46^1/_2$	12	$11^1/_2$	$12^1/_2$	14
$48^1/_2$	$13^1/_2$	13	14	$15^1/_2$

International shoe sizes

Australia		Japan		Mexico
M	**W**	**M**	**W**	
3	3$\frac{1}{2}$	21.5	21	-
3$\frac{1}{2}$	4	22	21.5	-
43$\frac{1}{2}$	4$\frac{1}{2}$	22.5	22	-
4$\frac{1}{2}$	5	23	22.5	-
5	5$\frac{1}{2}$	23.5	23	-
5$\frac{1}{2}$	6	24	23.5	4.5
6	6$\frac{1}{2}$	24.5	24	5
6$\frac{1}{2}$	7	25	24.5	5.5
7	7$\frac{1}{2}$	25.5	25	6
7$\frac{1}{2}$	8	26	25.5	6.5
8	8$\frac{1}{2}$	26.5	26	7
8$\frac{1}{2}$	9	27.5	27	7.5
10	10$\frac{1}{2}$	28.5	28	9
11	11$\frac{1}{2}$	29.5	29	10
12	12$\frac{1}{2}$	30.5	30	11
13$\frac{1}{2}$	14	31.5	31	12.5

The appeal of heels

Slipping on a pair of high heels forces a distinct anatomical shift that exaggerates the female form and metaphorically places it on a pedestal. Standing and walking on tiptoe causes the body's center of gravity to shift and reconfigure its balance. The lower back arches, the thighs power up, the ribs and bust move forward, the shoulder blades draw down and together. The spine lengthens and the chin lowers to accommodate an elevated sight line and gaze. From the outside, the silhouette of a woman in heels acquires more of an hourglass shape. Her shoulders appear broader, her waist looks slimmer, and her legs seem proportionately long.

A short woman may equate high heels with a feeling of empowerment and emancipation, because they conceivably enable her to look squarely into the eyes of a man she formally had to look up to and, in some cases, they may enable her to tower above him. It's impossible for a woman to cower in a pair of high heels because she is literally forced to take a stand.

» Heels and health

Podiatrists recommend low or mid-range heels but caution against wearing high heels for extended periods of time. High heels, more than any other style of shoe, need to support your foot so pumps and other enclosed styles make more sense than open-toed, strappy sandals, or backless mules. Choose uppers constructed from sturdy materials like

Words from the wise

Suzanne George, Handcrafted
shoemaker

» The perfect fit

Today's shoe industry caters to average feet and most
of us don't fit that bill. For example, if you have very
slender or wide feet then most manufacturers simply
can't accommodate you.

A well-fitting shoe feels comfortable and snug as
soon as you try it on. It never needs to be "broken in."
Its heel box has a degree of play; the opposite of
sloppy, its upper cradles your mid foot; your toes can
twinkle and your arch has noticeable support. Is the
shoe's heel centered under your heel so that your
weight is well distributed or is it placed too far back or
forward? It's okay if toes automatically splay in a pair
of high heels because there they play a supportive
role. And it's fine if there's not much wiggle room for
your heel in a boot that supports the ankle.

If you find an off-the-rack shoe that fits like a glove
buy more than one pair before they disappear forever
or have the original pair copied by a shoemaker.

leather, rather than flimsy fabrics that offer relatively little stability, and select shoe interiors that are smooth and soft with no jagged edges. Chunky heels and rounded toes offer more comfort than pointy toes and ice-pick-shaped heels.

Choose heels that contour to your arch, because they distribute your weight evenly rather than localize the weight on the ball of your foot. Make sure your high heels have shock-absorbing insoles or substantial soles, and choose high heels with a platform that reduces the pitch of the heel and positions the foot at a gentler angle. Customize high-heeled shoes by making them snug, rather than tight, with cushioning and padding.

» Walking in heels

The ability to walk in high heels doesn't come naturally to us all, and there are some tips for those who struggle:

- Wear high heels for events that don't involve a lot of walking, such as dinner parties or the theater, where you will be seated for lengths of time.
- Break in ultra-high heels by using mid-range heels as training wheels then graduate to higher heels over a period of time.
- When you wear high heels, always carry a pair of flats or kitten heels in case foot pain strikes and remove heels immediately if your toes begin to tingle or if any parts of your feet feel numb.
- Pamper your feet after an engagement with high heels by soaking them in warm, salted water that's infused with lavender oil.

» Bespoke and handmade

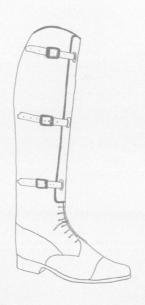

Customized shoes

Bespoke is to footwear what couture is to fashion. It's the top of the line of customization; the direct opposite of ready-to-wear and off-the-rack. But while couture combines a classic cut with a fashion forward outlook, bespoke footwear traditionally tended toward the conservative and staid, catering to the financially elite. Men who outfitted themselves in bespoke also had a personal Savile Row tailor and shirtmaker; women who owned bespoke likely had problematic or irregularly shaped feet and as they were unable to shop in regular stores they had to invest in quasi-orthopedic–looking shoes.

» Changing times

Nowadays bespoke women's footwear is far more stylish, and compared to the steep price of many top designers' styles, its cost isn't completely off the charts. Add to that a newfound appreciation for hand craftsmanship as well as a respect for the ancient tradition of shoemaking that qualifies it as an art. Women also have more confidence in their individual level of taste so the fickle "ins" and "outs" of the fashion industry don't stack up quite so favorably against the prospect of owning a unique pair of shoes that will conceivably remain vital for generations to come.

» Bespoke vs made-to-measure

Bespoke involves a team of artisans tailoring a shoe's pattern and crafting its upper onto a wooden last that's a three-dimensional replica of the customer's foot. The shoe takes several weeks or even months to complete because all of its components are hand cut and sewn, and because the shoe upper spends several weeks attached to the last before it is permanently molded.

Made-to-measure is less customized, rarely involves a unique last, and is generally a modification of a style that already exists in a shoemaker's portfolio where the customer weighs in on a shoe's color, finish, and surface detailing.

UNIQUE » RARE » LITTLE-KNOWN » **ULTIMATE EXPERT**

Ruby slippers The ruby slippers Judy Garland wore in the *Wizard of Oz* are amongst the most coveted pieces of movie memorabilia of all time. Gilbert Adrian, MGM's chief costumier, changed the original silver models to red and decorated them with more than 5,000 sequins to take advantage of the vibrancy of Technicolor. There's confusion about the number of pairs that originally existed but five cropped up in auction in recent years selling for between $15,000 and $666,000 (though a pair that came up for sale in 2011 failed to get its $2 million opening bid). To commemorate the film's 50th anniversary, jeweler Harry Winston crafted 25 carats of diamonds and 1,500 carats of rubies into US size-4 replicas. With a value of $3 million they rank as the most expensive shoes ever made.

Bespoke shoemakers

Alessandro Oteri

Via Borgospesso 8, Milan, Italy

Tel: +39 02 8908 2530, www.alessandroteri.com

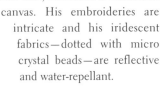

EXPERT *Essential* Born in Liguria, Oteri launched his own technique-driven line in 2004, featuring classic lines and evocative colors. His annual made-to-measure Anthology collection is sensible, restrained, and sophisticated and exemplifies his "elegance in motion" motto.

After their fitting, customers can choose between rich purples, mossy greens, and oceanic blues in a range of fabrics that includes chamois suede, pony skin, crocodile leather, and silk satin. Oteri's cloudy patent leather, constructed of overlapping suede with a sheer film, resembles a watercolor canvas. His embroideries are intricate and his iridescent fabrics—dotted with micro crystal beads—are reflective and water-repellant.

Anthology by Alessandro Oteri,
showcasing rich and glamorous colors

Anello & Davide

15 St. Albans Grove, Kensington, London, UK

Tel: +44 (0)20 7938 2255,
www.handmadeshoes.co.uk

Anello and Davide Gandolfi founded a dance and theatrical footwear company in Covent Garden in 1922 and went on to supply royalty, as well as stage and film celebrities, with superbly constructed classic footwear that married Italian flair to English craftsmanship.

Their customized service involves a team of specialists and it takes six to twelve months to deliver a shoe that is designed over the course of two fittings. The foot is measured and traced and a three-dimensional wooden form, or last, is carved to represent its individual contours.

Once the customer settles on a shoe style, the proportions of a standard pattern are adjusted and the grade and appropriate flexibility of leather is then chosen and cut. The upper is sewn together and fitted around the last where it stays for a period of time so that it can take on the characteristics of the customer's foot.

Final adjustments are made to the upper during a second fitting and then the pieces are attached to the soles and heels, and the shank is installed. Once all of the components are assembled, the shoes are cleaned, polished, and finished.

In the details

» Embroidery and embellishments

The wide use of machinery has reduced the extreme
labor intensity of applying baubles, pearls, or crystals
to uppers or vamps. Lavishly decorated shoes are no
longer rare items, with plenty of mass-produced lines
of flat sandals and evening shoes shimmering with
sequins or glass beads, classic pumps garnished with
clusters of pearls or rhinestones, and glittery prom
shoes all readily available at affordable prices.

Plenty of dressier shoes, however, often still
incorporate intricate embroidery, semiprecious
stones, or seed pearls into their decorative scheme,
and this calls for a skilled, detail-oriented application.
They are often constructed in Asian countries where
labor is more affordable and where manufacturers
rely on skilled craftspeople who are adept at intricate
handiwork and the end results are often comparable
to the pricier, European-produced versions created
by craftspeople who have a dressmaking background.

Opposite: Christian Louboutin Spring 2009
Haute Couture Collection

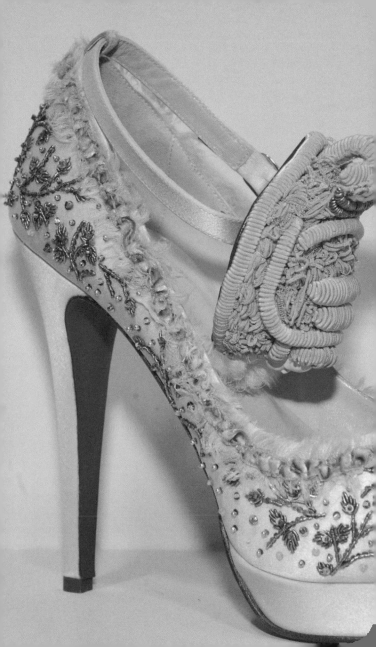

Anthony Delos

26, rue Marbeuf, Paris, France

Tel: +33 1 53 93 97 97, www.berluti.com

Delos perfected his bootmaking skills at the prestigious Compagnons de Devoir, an association that preserves traditional French craftsmanship, and at Lobb in Paris, so his classic women's shoes come from a *bottier* tradition that transcends fashion. Thanks to his orthopedics training he values detailed measurements, so he focuses on the idiosyncrasies of each client's anatomy—the foot's instep, tarsal, ball as well as its volume, boniness, and muscularity— before he selects the upper materials. He constructs a mock-up or trial shoe with a cork sole that he cuts and marks in an effort to achieve a perfect fit before he makes the real thing. Delos Bottier & Cie was acquired by Berluti in July 2013.

Caroline Groves

83 Jermyn Street, London, UK

Tel: +44 (0)20 7930 5385, www.carolinegroves.co.uk

EXPERT *Essential* The artful, customized shoes created by Groves in her Cotswold workshop are literal embodiments of her customers' personalities and dreams. An upper may incorporate a parakeet's wing; a heel may be covered in feathered embroidery or coated with Japanese lacquer.

After an initial fitting and exposure to a wide range of potential fabrics, customers evaluate a mocked-up shoe on their second visit, at which time they also consider alterations. They are then presented with the finished shoe on their third visit.

Groves' classically opulent styles include a wilted embroidered hydrangea, vintage shell buckles, French knots, or solid silver.

A customized Caroline Groves design, with parakeet wing uppers

By contrast, her Austere heeled lace-up, upholstered in ostrich or crocodile skin with understated hand-stitching, pays homage to pure form. She fits her customers in London and generally turns around the shoes within eight weeks.

Inventive designs

Unlike most of his counterparts, Salvatore Ferragamo was at his most inventive from the 1930s onward, when wartime shortages deprived the European shoe industry of its workaday materials. When economic sanctions caused the designer to run out of the German, steel, support shanks he inserted into his high heels, he invented cork wedges and encased them in brass fretwork for additional strength. When the Italian government cracked down on imports he sourced locally. He stacked wine corks to make heels and he built articulated soles out of wood and glass. Unphased by a leather shortage he wove shoe uppers from hemp, straw, woollen thread, candy wrappers, and fishing lines.

E. Vogel

19 Howard Street, New York, USA

Tel: 212 925 2460, www.vogelboots.com

One of the world's most distinguished bespoke equestrian bootmakers is located on four floors of an undistinguished building in lower Manhattan. Established in 1879 by Egidius Vogel, the firm is now in the hands of the family's fourth generation and riders and non-professionals alike covet their custom equestrian boots. Measurements can be taken at the store; alternatively they make house calls for New Yorkers or they send out-of-towners a measuring

An E. Vogel bespoke equestrian boot

kit that includes a DVD, a Ritz measuring stick, an illustrated guide, and material swatches. Their standard boots are known for their blemishless, imported calfskin uppers, leather lining, and stacked leather heels.

Kow Hoo Shoe Company

Shop 243, Prince's Building, 10 Chater Road, Hong Kong

Tel: +852 2523 0489, www.kowhoo.com.hk

Originally established in 1928, Kow Hoo is currently the oldest bespoke shoe shop in Hong Kong and the only one to maintain a tradition of preserving their

Words from the wise

Ruthie Davis, Shoe designer

» Flattering proportions

Always consider a shoe in the context of your overall shape, height and leg/torso proportion. It's ironic but if you're petite, a high heel with a thick platform may actually diminish your height if it appears to take up too much real estate and can make you look as if you're all shoe. Pick a style that flatters your assets: ankle straps draw attention to slim ankles; bootees accentuate toned calves and knee-high boots give form to shapeless legs.

Peep-toes should ideally reveal two toes and hint at a third and they're visually much kinder to unevenly shaped feet than completely open sandals. The golden rule for toe cleavage is that it never looks good when a foot has been squeezed into a shoe. Platforms are a woman's friend. A 2-inch platform on a shoe with a 5-inch-high heel reduces the shoe's pitch—as well as the foot's inclination—to a tolerable 3 inches.

customer's wooden lasts for at least seven years. They conduct personal fittings but also duplicate favorite shoes their customers send in.

In all cases a prototype shoe is mocked up from low-grade leather with a paper sole and cork heel, which is then mailed to the customer for a fit evaluation. Once it is returned to Hong Kong, all of the alterations are noted and then the actual shoe is crafted from European leathers or exotic skins and shipped to the customer, along with the original shoe. The entire process takes an average of six to eight months. Once the company has a customer's last on file, they are also able to duplicate shoes from a photograph.

Maison Steiger Bottier

35, Avenue Matignon, Paris, France

Tel: +33 1 47 42 29 32, www.waltersteiger.com

Following in the footsteps of his *bottier* father, Walter Steiger began designing shoe collections for fashion houses when he was 20 years old. Since then he has collaborated with the crème de la crème of fashion designers from Alaia to Ungaro and everyone in between.

After a career that spans more than six decades he has passed the mantle to his sons Paul and Giulio who now have a custom salon in the eighth *arrondissement*. Customers base their wants and needs on available styles, while shoemakers sit behind a smoked glass wall and work with lasts and an array of fluorescent leathers and exotic skins to produce shoes within six to eight weeks. The

Steiger style runs the gamut from low-key elegance to high-octane glamour that may flaunt transparent plastics, zippers, sequins, polka dots, or massive amounts of bling.

Terry De Havilland

330–336 Kingsland Road, London, UK

Tel: +44 (0)20 7254 4445, www.tdhcouture.com

EXPERT *Essential* Born into a London shoemaking family, de Havilland began cobbling in the 1950s after discovering a wedged pump his father had created in the 1940s. He has subsequently spent decades outfitting edgy fashionistas.

His patched snakeskin scaffolds shod the glam rock crowd; he collaborated with antiestablishment designers like Zandra Rhodes and Vivienne Westwood on their collections; he outfitted New Wavers with winkle picker stilettos and spent the 1990s surrounded by fetish and bondage boots. Rei Kawakuba and Alexander McQueen brought him back into public awareness and his colorful, theatrical retro styles feel more *au courant* now than ever before.

De Havilland women's custom service focuses on a wide selection of his

Terry de Havilland designs: "fantasy in footwear"

signature shapes and he loves customizing "honeymoon high heels" for "brides with attitude." Everything is measured, cut, sewn, and assembled in his informal workshop, so prices are comparatively moderate and the shoes are turned around within four weeks.

T. and F. Slack

32B St. Lawrence Terrace, London, UK

Tel: +44 (0)208 969 9100,
www.tandfslackshoemakers.com

Avid colorists Tim and Fiona Slack's radically fashionable shoes have endured since the 1970s. Their portfolio of classic reinterpretations includes multicolored suede loafers, vivid heeled brogues with cut-out sides, stripy ikat pumps, and penguin-inspired black-and-white laced wedges. In their Notting Hill store they offer a custom service that's demystified in a look book that houses 40 upper/welt combinations and an infinite combination of materials, colors, and soles. Customers try on their 3½ to 8½ (US size) samples, then keep refining their component choices until they achieve their desired style. The Slacks nurture young talent in their local factory and deliver shoes within one month.

» Luxury

Directors of fashion

Thanks to TV shows like *Sex and the City*, a handful of shoe designers who were once only known to devout shoe aficionados are now household names. Regularly profiled in society pages, they dictate the direction of shoe fashion, which is why they attract style scouts who document the launch of new collections as the first step in a knock-off process.

Fashion collections

All of the top fashion houses have their own eponymous collections of shoes that vary from season to season according to whatever styles and looks the designers are striving to achieve in their clothing.

Different leathers

The majority of women's luxury shoes are made from cow hide, but there are a number of other leathers that can be used as well. The unique softness and pliability inherent in deer and elk skins produce handsome and highly practical outdoor shoes; the nubby follicles in ostrich skin lends a pronounced contour to formal shoe uppers; while snakeskin lends texture and natural pattern to strappy sandals.

These include, to name just a few, Giorgio Armani, Yves Saint Laurent, Chanel, Marc Jacobs, Diane von Furstenberg, Lanvin, Balenciaga, Rick Owens, and Kate Spade.

In general, as far as fashion houses are concerned, shoes play second fiddle to the outfits, which is why they generally haven't been included here. There are some exceptions: the shoes that accompanied Alexander McQueen's spring/summer 2010 Paris collection upstaged the clothing and challenged footwear norms. Upholstered in animal skins and sequins, his extraordinary hybrid shoe/boots stood 10 inches tall and looked quasi-orthopedic as well as stunningly beautiful.

However, the main focus of the following pages is on those designers who primarily create shoes to be sold in their eponymous stores and, in many cases, in the e-boutiques on their websites. No matter where they primarily reside, top shoe designers spend a good deal of their time in European factories and workshops. The paparazzi zero in on their most photogenic or outrageous styles when they spot them on a celebrity, but all of these designers carry a broad range of luxury shoes that run the gamut from simple to showstopping.

Designers

Andrea Pfister

Massimo Bonini Showroom,
Via Montenapoleone 2/3, Milan, Italy

Tel: + 39 02 78 39 88, www.massimobonini.com

EXPERT *Essential* After studying design, Italian-born Pfister made shoes for the fashion houses of Patou and Lanvin and debuted his own label in 1965 when he opened his Parisian boutique. Baroque modern, feminine, eccentric, amusing, opulent, and enchanting, his themed collections produce shoes that might be mistaken for walking postcards. Features include uppers that resemble a saxophone, a martini glass, a mermaid, or a beach umbrella. A natural colorist, he employs exquisite gilt snakeskins, appliquéed embroideries, and multicolored suede, and is never influenced by trends. He prizes comfort and his motto is, "If a beautiful woman's feet hurt, she becomes ugly."

Andrea Pfister beach-
umbrella sandals

Anyi Lu

118 Hacienda Drive, Tiburon, CA, USA

Tel: 415 789 8891, www.anyilu.com

Anyi Lu's reinterpretations of iconic styles are designed in her Sausalito studio and hand-constructed in Italy.

The search for a stylish, comfortable, wedding shoe combined with a love of ballroom dancing led Lu to create collections of supportive, lightweight shoes with striking, slightly retro silhouettes. The customized, cushioned footbed in each pair of her flat and heeled shoes hugs the foot like a sock and simulates the flexibility of walking barefoot. Lu's classic twists include heeled ballet slippers, poppy-red loafers, leopard wedges, and ostrich pumps. Her feminized Oxfords have tassels and one version of her peep-toe slingbacks features bronzed lace while another combines taupe patent with nubby linen.

Bally

Via Industria 1, Caslano, Switzerland

Tel: +41 91 612 91 11, www.bally.com

From its humble, mid-19th century origins as a small, Swiss, family-run business Bally is now an international brand that's synonymous with quality materials and handcrafting. When Michael Herz and Graeme Fidler succeeded Brian Atwood as creative directors in 2011 they incorporated the firm's original essence into their first collection by dipping into the archives and re-conceptualizing a 1949 elastic upper, a metal heel from 1979, and an iconic 1940s Curling après-ski boot with a rubber sole, suede upper, and shearling lining. The character of subsequent perforated brogues, peep-toed pumps, and lacey T-straps is distinctly nostalgic, save for a futuristic upper that may be cut from ostrich skin, an ice pick-type heel, or a super-chic wedge.

Beatrix Ong

4 Burlington Arcade, Mayfair, London, UK

Tel: +44 (0)207 499 4089, www.beatrixong.com

Sculptural art and function meet in Ong's collection, with uppers that are elegantly fanned, delicately laced, or feature neat origami detailing. Then there are also her sensuous 1930s-inspired platforms, her chic flat-as-a-pancake slides, and her signature asymmetrical, high-heeled Mary Janes. Brought up in Hong Kong, she studied at Central Saint Martins, F.I.T., and Cordwainers and became the creative director of Jimmy Choo (see page 61) at the stunningly young age of 22. She has collaborated with a long list of clothing designers as well as brands such as Nike, Aquascutum, and Pringle, and she launched her own line in 2002.

Brian Atwood

Piazzale Susa 2, Milan, Italy

Tel: +39 02 8739 3596, www.brianatwood.com

Launched in 2001 and distinguished by its come-hither glamour, Brian Atwood's line is a favorite of Hollywood starlets. Born in Chicago, Atwood studied art and architecture, graduated from New York's Fashion Institute of Technology, and then met Gianni Versace while modeling in Europe. A period of designing accessories for the Versus and Versace labels followed before he established his own line. His bold, eye-catching, hyper-feminine silhouettes are paparazzi magnets on international red carpets. A pump may have a grosgrain ribbon trim, an

Words from the wise

Llorainne Neithardt, Shoe artist and teacher, Shoe Fine Art

» Expressing your personality

Women's shoes are not just basic, functional objects, they are also agents of mystery that are steeped in psychology, symbolism, and sexuality. So choosing a shoe is more than just matching your outfit, it's about expressing your personality too.

When I teach, I show how it's possible to tap into our fantasies, dreams, and imaginations in order to create a shoe that embodies our persona. More than any other accessory or piece of clothing, a shoe's design—its texture, color, height, proportion, and shape—gives off subliminal messages about how we perceive ourselves and how we want the world to perceive us. That's why we have such an intimate, complex relationship with our shoes.

Statistically women tend to sacrifice comfort for style but I espouse the belief that a successful shoe makes feet feel as alive and beautiful as they look. I also challenge the notion that the higher the heel, the sexier the shoe, because I've seen kitten heels that have made grown men quiver!

oversized polka-dot upper, or gold buckle fastenings and an average heel height of 5 inches with occasional heels soaring to 6.5 inches. A pair of Atwood's purple suede espadrilles feature striped wedges, while a platform bootee, entirely covered with fringe, might pay homage to a shaggy dog.

Bruno Frisoni

34, rue de Grenelle, Paris, France

Tel: +33 142 84 1230, www.brunofrisoni.com

EXPERT *Essential* Sensual elegance characterizes Frisoni's collection of highly feminine, skinny, high-heeled shoes, where a strong sense of architecture marries dressmaker details. One sandal's upper resembles intertwining garter belts while another looks like a folded straw purse. On another vamp, slinky black ribbons hold thick bands of black elastic in place.

While he currently designs for his own label, he is also the creative director of the Parisian house of Roger Vivier where he tweaks and reinterprets the maestro designer's archival silhouettes, using a range of cut velvets, hand embroideries, and metallic threads.

Dressmaker details often feature on Frisoni's collections

Camilla Skovgaard

15 Lots Road, Unit 20, London, UK

Tel: +44 (0)207 310 8446,
www.camillaskovgaard.com

This Danish designer already had a career in women's couture before she attended Cordwainers and London's Royal College of Art, so it wasn't a total surprise when Saks Fifth Avenue bought her first collection of footwear before she'd even graduated. The label she introduced in 2006 has won several awards for its lofty, stark, and architectural styles, prompting one journalist to refer to her as the Arne Jacobsen of couture. She produces in China using all Italian materials, and a number of her high ankle boots have recognizable jagged soles while some uppers are layered under braided twill trim.

Casadei

Via Sant'Andrea 1, Milan, Italy

Tel: +39 02 76 31 82 93, www.casadei.com

In 1964 Cesare Casadei became the creative head of the firm his family founded in 1958. Like his parents before him, he still designs finely crafted, hyper-feminine shoes that are indisputably handcrafted in Italy. The heels of his peep-toed, vertiginous slingbacks are often encrusted with crystals and despite their sturdiness have been described as "impossibly beautiful." His naked-looking, spaghetti-strapped, flat sandals often resemble bracelets and corsages, which is one reason he attracts a loyal following of Hollywood celebrities.

Charlotte Olympia

56 Maddox Street, London, UK

Tel: +44 (0)207 499 0145,
www.charlotteolympia.com

Half Brazilian, half English, Charlotte Olympia Dellal graduated from Cordwainers in 2004 and launched her own line three years later. She cites 1940s glamour as one of her inspirations, vaudeville as another, and while the silhouettes of her boots, pumps, and T-straps are simple, her tasseled, hooped, and braided trims are overtly theatrical. She uses kimono fabrics, cork, or large-scale leopard freely and she's bold and confident with color. Her heels have been described as vertigo inducing and her flats are paper thin. She stamps her logo—a gold spiderweb—onto the sole of each one of her shoes.

Christian Louboutin

19, rue Jean-Jacques Rousseau, Paris, France

Tel: +33 1 42 36 05 31,
www.christianlouboutin.com

The son of a cabinetmaker, Louboutin began sketching shoes in his teens. He abandoned school, dabbled in acting, and eventually brought his portfolio of shoe sketches to a few fashion houses, including Charles Jourdan who gave him a job. Subsequently he became an apprentice at Roger Vivier's atelier, sold his designs to Maud Frizon, Chanel, and Yves Saint Laurent, and eventually opened his first boutique in Paris in 1991.

His standard, staggeringly high 5-inch heels exemplify his love of the Folies Bergeres (a Parisian music hall established in 1869) and are invariably a vehicle to showcase the inner arch contour which, in his eyes, qualifies as the sexiest line of a woman's foot.

As if acknowledging the inner showgirl in every woman, he hopes the jeweled straps, exaggerated bows, and coquettish feathers on his vamps "slow women down and give them a sexier gait." Determined that his shoes leave a lasting impression

UNIQUE » RARE » LITTLE-KNOWN » **ULTIMATE EXPERT**

Naked shoes On occasion, designers have marketed barely-there shoes that feel completely flat. In 1947, Salvatore Ferragamo created a sandal with an upper constructed from translucent nylon fishing line for Dior's frothy New Look crinoline skirts. According to the modest and thrifty post World War II mentality, its nakedness and price were overtly frivolous and shocking (it cost the same as a four-ton bag of coal). In 1957, Beth Levin went a step further when she attached surgical pads to a heeled top sole that literally had no upper. Her No Shoes were sold with a bottle of adhesive so that the sole of each "shoe" could be adhered to the skin of the wearer's bare sole. There were few buyers, and critics dismissed the experiment.

he lacquers their soles bright red and the top lifts of his heels often leave rosette imprints.

Emma Hope

207 Westbourne Grove, London, UK

Tel: +44 (0)207 792 7800, www.emmahope.com

Emma Hope grew up in Singapore and London, studied at Cordwainers alongside Patrick Cox, Christine Ahrens, and Elizabeth Stuart-Smith, and sold her first collection in 1984. Over the years she has worked with designers including Jean Muir, John Flett, Paul Smith, and Anna Sui. Influenced by her collection of vintage bags and gloves, she incorporates traditional sewing techniques into the velvet, suede, and glove leather in her pumps and flats, which are handcrafted in Florence. Her calf-lined sneakers, cut from pony skin or python, feel decidedly old school.

Ernesto Esposito

Via Santa Caterina a Chiaia 20, Naples, Italy

Tel +39 081 42 38 325,
www.ernestoespositoshoes.com

EXPERT *Essential* Esposito worked alongside maestro Sergio Rossi for 15 years and then spent a decade with Marc Jacobs as well as stints with Chloe, Sonia Rykiel, and Louis Vuitton. Strongly influenced by contemporary art, he often builds his shapes around color or combines several patterns as if his canvas is never confined literally to the shoe itself: a ballet slipper has gold lamé, leopard, and pink sections with a tiger-print toecap; the spaghetti-

strap upper of a high-heeled sandal is multicolored, while its back and T-strap are pink leopard. His shoes are made in Naples at the Apema factory, which also makes his Lerre label.

Ernesto Esposito high heel with spaghetti-strap upper

Estelle Yomeda

4, rue de Normandie, Paris, France

Tel: +33 1 44 59 80 33, www.estelleyomeda.com

Trained as a visual artist, Estelle Yomeda opened her Parisian boutique in 2007 and her collections have a strong vintage feel. She's adept at combining comfort and fantasy in her sandals and boots by using unexpected, retro-feminine colors. Her collections feel handcrafted and always flatter the line of the leg. A chunky heeled sandal with solid ankle straps could easily pass for a dance shoe, while linen and glitter happily coexist on a low, 1950s-style pump.

Fendi

Via Flaminia 1068, Rome, Italy

Tel: +39 06 33 45 01, www.fendi.com

In 1925, newlyweds Adele and Edoardo Fendi sold leather and fur handbags from a humble store in Rome. The company is now one of Italy's most celebrated luxury brands. Currently art directed by Silvia Venturini Fendi and Karl Lagerfeld, who first introduced the double F logo in 1965, the brand caters to women who covet well-crafted, high-fashion footwear from ballet slippers, to wide, Russian-cut boots and strappy platform pumps. The range of styles is detail-orientated, combining refined leather, goatskin, and fur elements, while items such as color-blocked, corset-laced ankle boots promote hyper-modern femininity.

Ferragamo

4r–14r, Via dei Tornabuoni, Florence, Italy

Tel: +39 055 292 123, www.ferragamo.com

Salvatore Ferragamo made his first shoe when he was nine, and he went on to become one of the most prolific, innovative, and original designers of the 20th century. Born near Naples, a stint in Hollywood earned him the title of "shoemaker to the stars," and his company is still revered for its beautifully crafted shoes. Massimiliano Gornetti became its creative director in 2010, and his updates on Ferragamo's iconic styles include houndstooth stilettos, metal-heeled sandals, and peep-toed pumps, all of which blend the venerable with the fresh.

Gianvito Rossi

Via Santo Spirito, 7, Milan, Italy

Tel: +39 02 76 28 09 88, www.gianvitorossi.com

Gianvito Rossi worked alongside his legendary father, Sergio, for over twenty years and launched his own line in 2006. He chooses sensuous materials like stretch silk, Karung snakeskin, and waved suede to create shoes that are elegant, airy, and ultra feminine whether they are flat, have kitten heels, or 5-inch wedges. His silhouettes come across as spare, weightless, and refined and belie how much craftsmanship they contain. Pearls cascade from the heels of a black satin pump; dotted rows of crystals animate a Lucite wedge; a sandal upper is entirely composed of a red leather spiderweb. His lightweight, carbon, high-heel collection would resemble a portfolio of stick drawings if it weren't for a gold lamé ruffle here or an oversized black pompom there.

Giuseppe Zanotti

Via Montenapoleone, 18, Milan, Italy

Tel: +39 02 784 827,
www.giuseppezanottidesign.com

Born close to Rimini in an Adriatic town known mainly for its shoe manufacturing, Zanotti's collaborations with local artisans brought his footwear to the attention of major fashion houses, from Balmain to Proenza Schouler. He describes his designs as adornments rather than coverings and the inventory that filled the Milan boutique he opened in 2000 exemplified just that. Inspired by art, cinema, and music he still creates high pumps in bright primary colors, strappy snakeskin bootees with concealed platforms, and low sandals whose crystal-encrusted suede cradles the ankle.

Gucci

Via Montenapoleone 5-7, Milan, Italy

Tel: +39 02 771 271, www.gucci.com

Gucci, the world-renowned purveyor of goods and luggage, is currently part of PPR SA, a French

» Pointed toes

Apart from some recently invented high-concept
sneakers, shoe design never originated from a foot's
anatomical outline. In other words there was never a
time when footwear literally fit like a glove. Shoes,
instead, were always modeled after a stylized or
idealized form. For some reason, shoes with pointed
toes—a shape that bears no resemblance whatsoever to
a footprint—have always held a place of prominence in
the fashion world. As far back as the 10th century,
Chinese foot binding molded women's feet and toes in
order to achieve an exaggerated point. Poulaines,
pointed shoes worn by French nobility in medieval
times, had no such long-term physical deformation but
they caused absolute havoc on the battlefield when
they were imitated in armor. Winklepickers became
fashionable in 1950s when rock 'n' rollers and Teddy
Girls began wearing them and, to this day, a pointed-
toed stiletto is still considered to be THE shoe among
fashion-conscious women.

Opposite: Pointed toes are always fashionable,
although they bear no resemblance to the shape of a foot

group that also owns Bottega Veneta, Yves Saint Laurent, and Alexander McQueen. Its interlocking monogrammed loafers are a perennial, unisex calling card for exclusivity and wealth. Founded in Florence in 1921, the brand boasts an impressive list of former creative directors including Geoffrey Beene, Calvin Klein, and Tom Ford, who brought a sultry, raw sexiness to the brand's aristocratic image. His protégé Frida Giannini currently designs sophisticated, leggy footwear that appeals to a youthful clientele. She relies heavily on archival styles and might base a collection on the firm's equestrian heritage or remove the saccharine from a classic 1940s vintage floral pattern by applying it to a sexy, high-heeled upper.

Jan Jansen

Rokin 42, KT Amsterdam, The Netherlands

Tel: +31 20 810 0523, www.janjansenshoes.com

EXPERT
Essential
Born in 1941 the son of a shoe salesman, this Amsterdam-based designer has produced collections of footwear in limited editions, since the 1960s. His renowned technical innovations—floating, heelless wedges; metallic rod heels that coil like snakes—are perfectly proportioned interplays between the last, heel, and sole. His simple reinterpretation of the classic Dutch clompen contrasts with the

Jan Jansen's technical innovations:
a cantilevered shoe

knee-high boots that serve as canvases for the distinctive colors and sumptuous fabrics his wife, Tonny, selects. An everyday Jansen shoe may feature bamboo, toile de jouy, plexiglass, python, metallic goat, or flame-shaped silver kid.

Jimmy Choo

32 Sloane Street, London, UK

Tel +44 (0)207 823 1051, www.jimmychoo.com

Born in Malaysia into a family of shoemakers, Choo came up with his first shoe design at age 11. He graduated from Cordwainers and worked out of an old factory in the East of London. In 1988, this is where *Vogue* discovered him, at his workbench, surrounded by piles of stunning 4-inch party heels. Patronage from Diana, Princess of Wales followed a couple of years later and secured the status factor of the brand that is still synonymous with sumptuous materials, pointed toes, stiletto heels, and strappy high sandals. Former accessories editor Tamara Mellon invested in Choo and bought the designer out in 2001, but she still channels his creativity and is responsible for the brand becoming a household name.

Joseph Azagury

73 Knightsbridge, London, UK

Tel: +44 (0)207 259 6887, www.josephazagury.com

Born in Morocco, Azagury sold shoes in Harrods' Rayne department while he learned how to cobble at Cordwainers College. After working in Spain, Italy, and the United States, he established his own label in 1990, in London, where he still draws and sculpts shoes that are then constructed in Italy. Early in his career he was thought of as the affordable Blahnik but nowadays his signature silhouettes are strongly individual and exemplified in their sexy, slightly retro, simple, flowing lines and manageably high heels in crêpe satin, patent leather, and natural cork. Bridesmaids favor his white satin pumps and Swarovski crystal sandals.

Julia Lundsten

Universal House, 251 Tottenham Court Road, London, UK

Tel: +44 (0)7894 904 315, www.finsk.com

Finnish designer Julia Lundsten won the prestigious Manolo Blahnik award two years in a row because he found her footwear to be "exquisite, divine, and perfect." She launched her Finsk line in 2004 and has consulted with clothing brands like Kurt Geiger, Top Shop, and Jaeger. Rather than fashion, she looks to architecture and furniture for inspiration and sees a shoe's heel and sole as the legs, and its upper as the seat of a chair. Consequently, her structured, scaffold-like shoes have earned her the "Eames of footwear" description. Made in Brazil from local woods and leather that are by-products of other industries, her most recognizable shoe—a zippered pump that morphs into a cleaved platform—is deceptively comfortable.

The Finsk line is known for its structured shoes

Laurence Dacade

17, rue Duphot, Paris, France

Tel: +33 9 65 34 15 99, www.laurence-dacade.com

Paris-based Dacade defines her average client as an "androgynous woman who is a femme fatale at night." She made her first pair of shoes at age 14, trained at the AFPIC School and launched her own label in 2003. After designing for Givenchy for five years, she shot into the spotlight with a pair of pistol-heeled stilettos that came out of her collaboration with Karl Lagerfeld for Chanel's 2009 Cruise collection. She innately understands construction and, surprisingly, values comfort. An inveterate traveler she claims to conceptualize most of her cool, sensual, slightly nostalgic rock-chick footwear while waiting for trains and planes.

Liam Fahy

Studio 3, 7 Milton Road, Highgate, UK

www.liamfahy.com

EXPERT *Essential* Raised on a Zimbabwe snake farm, Fahy made his first shoe out of an old car tire. The conceptual footwear he conceived while studying at the De Montfort University won him awards. After graduating in 2006, he designed sports shoes, but later decided to turn his back on the mass sneaker industry and his award-winning women's footwear led him to become a protégé of Rupert Sanderson. He works out of a Venice factory that upholds age-old production methods and each pair of his shoes take two days to craft. His elegant collections utilize haired calf, camoscio, metallic water snake, and nabuk python skins. Their timeless silhouettes are thought to be as endurable as Chanel perfume. The fronts of his signature 4-inch heels hide a tiny platform that makes the wearer look as if her feet aren't touching the floor. All of his shoes have his signature nickel embedded in their sole.

A Liam Fahy
snakeskin slingback

Louis Vuitton

101, avenue des Champs-Elysées, Paris, France

Tel: +33 1 45 49 62 30, www.louisvuitton.com

The Louis Vuitton label and its iconic LV monogram ranks as the most counterfeited brand of wallets, bags, luggage, and footwear of all time. It was founded in 1854 and is currently owned by LMVH, with clothing designer Marc Jacobs at its helm. Jacobs' edgy, youthful aesthetic yields shoes with conventional styles that are deliciously provocative. A patent leather Oh Really pump with classic lines features a provocative gold padlock dangling from its back; a pair of pastel-colored alligator pumps flaunt a pointed silver toecap; a cork wedge, constructed from the firm's iconic signature canvas, sports an oversized patent bow on its vamp; while a stiletto-heeled sandal crafted from a single satin lace forms a birdcage-like construction as it encloses the foot.

Manolo Blahnik

49–51, Old Church Street, London, UK

Tel: +44 (0)207 352 8622,
www.manoloblahnik.com

Dismissing platforms as "surgical things" Manolo Blahnik favors spiky mules, pointy toes, and refined uppers that he may top off with a fistful of pearls or a whimsical strand of miniature rosettes. In the early 1970s, style maven Diana Vreeland saw his portfolio of stage set drawings and told him to switch professions and "go make shoes." Thanks to jewel-

The first celebrity shoe designer

The son of a shoemaker, Andre Perugia opened his first shop in Naples in 1909, at the age of 16. After World War I, the couturier Paul Poiret introduced him to Paris and an illustrious clientele list. Perugia had an uncanny way of capturing a woman's personality traits in a turban-shaped upper, a corkscrew heel, or a masked vamp. Legends like Gloria Swanson and Josephine Baker saw his shoes as three-dimensional portraits. He collaborated with Elsa Schiaparelli, designed under the Rayne label in England and the I. Miller label in the United States, and designed for Charles Jourdan. He catered to the crème de la crème of the fashion and entertainment worlds but he liked to say that he preferred to talk to his shoes rather than his clients.

toned silks, metallic tapestries, and complex embroideries his shoes still ooze theatrical flair as they tap into fantasy and reference costume history. He attained royalty status after his adrenalin-inducing high heels starred in *Sex and the City*, and declared Manolos to be the prerequisite shoe for any woman stepping out of a limo.

Max Kibardin

Via Solferino, 3, Milan, Italy

Tel: +39 02 36 55 55 47, www.maxkibardin.com

Born in Siberia, Kibardin studied architecture in Moscow before moving to Paris and then Milan, where he worked for the fashion houses of Alberto Biani and Pollini. He originated his own shoe label in 2004 and has collaborated with Pringle of Scotland and Chado Ralph Rucci.

He fondly remembers observing his grandfather handcrafting footwear in Georgia and as a result always tries to infuse emotions into his designs. Inspired by poems, dreams, ballets, movies, 1990s minimalism, and matinee idol glamour, he endeavors to "exalt the female form." He is the creative director for Bruno Magli, the venerable Milanese firm.

Kibardin's shoes are often a marriage between excess and moderation. From the front, an austere looking peep-toed black pump doesn't reveal the chiffon frill that runs down the entire length of its heel; the shaft of a neon green bootee is piled high with five layers of thick fringe; while an open, high-heeled sandal holds the foot in place with rows of pink flowers.

Michel Perry

243, rue Saint Honoré, Paris, France

Tel: +33 1 42 84 12 45, www.michelperry.com

Born in 1952, Perry dreamed of becoming a painter before he joined his family's footwear distribution business. At first he designed shoes reluctantly, until he began to see them as a valid means of artistic expression—he has described his lines as "lingerie you can see." He launched his own brand in 1987 and still feels influenced by English pop rock, culture, and humor of that period, as well as the libertine spirit of 18th-century France. He has designed countless collections for runway shows and is currently the creative director of French master shoemaker J. M. Weston. In recent seasons classic met cartoon in a pair of mid-heeled pumps that vibrate with oversize yellow polka dots; ankle strapped platforms recall Betty Boop; Chinese fastenings and black tassels ornament a pair of gold platform lace-ups; and a generous sheepskin collar sits at the throat vamp of a pair of tall bootees.

Minna Parikka

Bulevardi 24, Helsinki, Finland

Tel: +358 9 667 554,
www.minnaparikkashop.com

 Parikka designed her first shoe at the age of 15. She equates the realization that she

Minna Parikka pink Siouxsie shoes

could have a career making footwear with being struck by lightning. After studying and working in Europe for six years, she returned to her native Helsinki in 2005 and proceeded to launch her eponymous label.

Her feminine styling is nostalgic, and vintage undergarment components like black lace and corsetry crop up on her strappy sandals and pumps. Her influences include Ferragamo, Vivier, and Thea Cadabra who thought of her footwear as vehicles to articulate sweet provocations and feminist statements. Parikka uses color boldly, so purple, deep turquoise, and lipstick reds are familiar on her pumps, high boots, and ballet flats.

Natacha Marro

10 Manor road, Stoke Newington, London, UK

Tel: +44 (0)208 802 0841, www.natachamarro.com

Marro grew up in Nice and moved to London where she studied at Cordwainers, and went on to open her first shop in 2000. "It all clicked when I started making shoes," she said. "With shoes, I was innocent." She's now a darling designer of fashion magazines, pop divas, and theatrical costumiers; she has a made-to-measure clientele and season after season her shoes upstage the fashion catwalks. The sky-high heels, peep-toes, and heavy lacing she favors reference fetish wear but there's humor and irony in her burlesque striped bootees and her pearl glitter open-heeled staggerers.

Nicholas Kirkwood

5 Mount Street, London, UK

Tel: +44 (0)207 290 1404,
www.nicholaskirkwood.com

Nicholas Kirkwood
stiletto platform,
covered in neon lace

 British born
Kirkwood's
debut 2005 collection of
5-inch-high, architectural
platforms resulted in commissions
from Chloe, Rodarte, Alberta
Ferreti, and Pollini. His traditional
craftsmanship has a distinct edge. He refers to his
wedge soles as "motion platforms" and he avoids pointy
toes—his signature hybrid stiletto/platform is both
clunky and sexy. His recent brightly colored collections
feature details such as neon lace and rose-shaped
uppers, celebrating a playful feminism. He is currently
striving to perfect the holy grail of footwear—a
comfortable 2- to 3-inch heel that exudes the same
excitement as his 5-inch high-heeled totters.

069

Nicole Brundage

Via Piranesi, 4, Milan, Italy

Tel: +39 02 36 75 49 50, www.bybrundage.com

Brundage moved to Milan from San Antonio,
Texas to study fashion, and while there she
interned for Giorgio Armani. She subsequently
collaborated with Manolo Blahnik while working
with Zac Posen and went on to launch her own line
in 2006. She uses stressed and patent leathers,
satin, suede, and elastic strapping to form the
uppers of her slinky pumps and her colors—dove

gray, pearlized putty, light tan—are sophisticated and elegant. Her work often acknowledges an aesthetic debt to her favorite designers, Roger Vivier and Jan Jansen.

Peter Fox

Tel: 212 431 7426, www.peterfox.com

Peter Fox's beautifully constructed modernized versions of period shoes are only available on the Internet. His silk, Louis-heeled pumps and Mary Janes are particularly loved by brides. Fox studied sculpture and then worked in Harrods' shoe department before he became a shoe apprentice and his shoes are now bench-made in Italy.

Pierre Hardy

9–11 place du Palais Bourbon, Paris, France

Tel: +33 1 45 55 00 67, www.pierrehardy.com

EXPERT *Essential* Born and raised in Paris, Hardy studied dance while he completed his fine arts degree. In 1987 he revitalized Christian Dior and subsequently became the creative director of Hermès. He started his own line in 1999 and is known for his finely proportioned, modernist styles. In a collection for Balenciaga he created futuristic and playful high-heeled shoes that looked as if they were assembled from a kit of multicolored robot components. His own collections are just as

Multicolored Balenciaga stiletto designed by Hardy

graphic, but they celebrate the sumptuousness of the materials and colors he chooses. The capsule collection he designed for the Gap store demonstrated his ability to inject flair into the generic.

Prada

Galleria Vittorio Emanuele II, 63/65, Milan, Italy

Tel: +39 02 87 69 79, www.prada.com

Prada started life in 1913 as a small Milanese leather goods store run by Mario Prada and his brother Martino. His granddaughter, Miuccia, joined the company in 1970 and eight years later introduced generic, nylon backpacks that slowly elevated the brand to its current, internationally celebrated status.

Footwear followed in 1984 and like the brand's clothing it is both elegant and funky and marries sophistication with urban grit. Her secondary Miu Miu line appeals, in the designer's words, to "the bad girls I knew at school, the ones I envied." Shoes from both brands are influential, highly copied, and truly original. Platform sandals may be clunky and cartoonish, while mid-heeled pumps are downright conservative except for their narrowly sliced heel, and her Oxfords are surprisingly formal even with their integrated, injection-molded sole.

Raphael Young

23, rue Jean-Jacques Rousseau, Paris, France

Tel: +33 6 64 52 87 06, www.raphaelyoung.com

Raphael Young created his first pair of shoes at the age of 14 under the guidance of his uncle, famed *bottier*, Alexandre Narcy. Born in Seoul, Young first worked for Yves Saint Laurent before introducing his own label in 2007.

He spices up traditional craftsmanship with technical brilliance—such as his mother-of-pearl upholstered stilettos, with their wedged uppers, which have been called "quasi-futuristic and exquisitely beautiful." His patented R-Flex pump is made from malleable rubber and leather soles with latex injected under the ball of the foot, while structural steel inserts prevent twisted ankles. "Most designers draw and then construct the shoe. I sketch, build the shoe, and then take it apart again to create something new," he says. "Shoes are alive, nourished through material research and technological innovation."

Rene Caovilla

Via S. Andrea, 2, Milan, Italy

Tel: +39 02 7640 6404, www.renecaovilla.com

Caovilla comes from a Riviera del Brenta shoemaking family and took over the business in the early 1960s. A decade later he was collaborating with couturiers like Chanel, Valentino, and Christian Dior, who coveted his opulent aesthetic.

Each one of his evening shoes is fully capable of illustrating a fairy tale. A pair of crystallized lace butterflies perch on a strappy, black suede sandal; a tricolor of snakeskin straps form a lattice for an open flower; a black-and-white, high-stepping shoe might have jumped off the keys of a grand piano; and the hanging gemstones encrusting a flat sandal look like an upside-down tiara.

Words from the wise

Raul Ojeda, Don Ville Bespoke Shoemakers

» Weight distribution

When it comes to shoes, fashion is fun, but fit is all important. At one time, a shoemaker was considered to be as important as a doctor because both professions are built around promoting good health. Look at shoes as if they are a part of your anatomy, responsible for accommodating your foot and supporting your body. Evaluate whether your entire weight is distributed evenly across your feet, as this is connected to having a healthy back and good posture.

Even the best shoemaker can't tailor a shoe with a 5-inch-high heel to make it as comfortable as a Nike sneaker, so try to have realistic expectations about the level of relief you can expect from a very fashion forward shoe. If you come to terms with your particular foot shape and anatomy, you may end up dismissing certain styles because they don't promote a feeling of well-being or because they're painful or unflattering. Many of my customers don't consider customized, made-to-measure bridal shoes to be an extravagance, but I wish they would pamper their feet like that every day of the year.

Robert Clergerie

5, rue du Cherche-Midi, Paris, France

Tel: +33 1 45 48 75 47, www.robertclergerie.com

Born in Paris in 1934, Clergerie began designing his own line of footwear in 1981 by feminizing a man's lace-up Oxford. This style still crops up in his current lines in a slew of variations. He stresses comfort in all of his designs so he's liable to use stretchy suede and malleable leather, which conform to the foot on his platforms, boots, and raffia-soled lace-ups. He rarely decorates his footwear so they come across as exercises in materiality and shape. They are made in Romans, in the southeast of France.

Rodolphe Menudier

14 rue de Castiglione, Paris, France

Tel: +33 1 42 60 86 27,
www.rodolphemenudier.com

Menudier's label came into existence in 1994 and it is perennially reminiscent of Roger Vivier, Perugia, and Ferragamo for its resolved proportions, sophisticated materiality, and seductive coloration. He has collaborated with Balenciaga, Chanel, Chloe, Lacroix, Paco Rabane, and Dior, and his motto is "step by step." His aesthetic has been described as neopunk due to his prolific use of zippers and electric, shimmery patent leathers. His 5-inch-high cuffed ankle boots may make use of aluminum or hologram plastic but they still come across as ultra-feminine and luxurious.

Rupert Sanderson

19 Bruton Place, London, UK

Tel: +44 (0)207 491 2260,
www.rupertsanderson.com

A pair of Rupert Sanderson leopard wedge pumps, with gold heel

Sanderson left a failed career in advertising to enroll at Cordwainers College in London and during the summer hiatus toured as much of Italy's shoemaking region as possible. After graduation he worked for Bruno Magli and Sergio Rossi, where he put his "less is more" credo into practice.

In his opinion, a shoe fails if it doesn't flatter the leg, so he devotes time to perfecting his lines and even names every shoe he creates after types of daffodil. He currently designs all the shoes for Karl Lagerfeld's catwalks and writes a weekly blog for British *Vogue*. His pink heeled "brothel creepers" epitomize elegance; his black-and-white, high shoe-boots look sexy and devout all at the same time; and his leopard pumps are the height of respectability.

Ruthie Davis

Tel: 212 675 2269, www.ruthiedavis.com

EXPERT *Essential* Former design director for Reebok, Tommy Hilfiger, and Ugg, Ruthie Davis started her own line in 2005, making shoes from titanium, chrome, graphite, and carbon fiber. Her collections are always dramatic. In bright colors, a

punked up heel that's lined with spikes comes across as playful; a bubble-gum pink high heel on a multibanded Mary Jane reads as innocent bondage; a ballerina flat covered with nail heads reads as prickly rather than lethal. The bands of colors on her sneakers are commonly seen as instant mood elevators.

Ruthie Davis' Graffiti Mondrian pump

Sergio Rossi

Via Pontaccio 13, Milan, Italy

Tel: +39 02 763 2081, www.sergiorossi.com

Francesco Russo is the creative director of Sergio Rossi and he creates footwear that exudes feminine strength. He joined Yves Saint Laurent in 2000, where he guarded the house's sexy, timeless legacy, before going on to design for Miu Miu and Costume National. "The perfect shoe should elongate the leg and flatter the most sensual aspect of the foot, it should excite the wearer and the watcher," he says.

His high-heeled, neon-yellow leather or rose-colored snakeskin sandals are deceptively comfortable; laser-cut filigree pumps are laden with crystals but look buoyant; a mid-calf sandal laces up like a corset; retro-looking platforms burst with printed flowers; an upper combines python skin and orange PVC, and over-the-knee boots feature studded detailing, open toes, and a 4-inch chopstick-shaped heel.

Stuart Weitzman

675 5th Avenue, New York, USA

Tel: 212 759 1570, www.stuartweitzman.com

Stuart Weitzman began designing shoes for his father's Massachusetts business in the early 1960s when he was in his twenties. His shoes are now part-spectacle part-sculpture and he likes to envision them glamorously adoring and adorning a woman's

Stilettos

No one designer was responsible for inventing the stiletto heel. Andre Perugia had already perfected a thin high heel in the 1940s, while in the 1950s Roger Vivier resolved his version of the stiletto about the time Salvatore Ferragamo perfected his comfortable high heel in Italy. Gina, a London firm headed by Mehmet Kurdash, first encased an aluminum spigot inside leather and produced a pencil-like heel that was stable and strong. They were called "needle heels" in France and "five cents" in Hong Kong, due to the size of the impression left by the heel tip. A number of people spoke out against the stiletto, including doctors and ministers, while public building administrators banned them in case they pockmarked their lobby floors.

foot. He continually experiments with materials as widely diverse as vinyl wallpaper and 24-carat gold, and he embellishes his shoes with chromed pillared heels, layered woods, bamboo, cork, gemstones, and hand-set crystals. His shoes are made in southern Spain and his stores routinely carry styles in four widths, from super slim to wide.

Walter Steiger

83, Faubourg St Honoré, Paris, France

Tel: +33 1 42 66 65 08, www.waltersteiger.com

Walter Steiger apprenticed with his shoemaker father in Switzerland from the age of 15, before leaving for Paris and London where his creations finished off Mary Quant's geometric outfits. He moved to Paris to design for Ungaro, opened his first boutique in 1974, and eight years later set up shop on Park Avenue while supplying runway shoes for Bill Blass, Oscar de la Renta, and Calvin Klein.

His subsequent collections for Azzadine Alaia, Helmut Lang, Karl Lagerfeld, Claude Montana, Kenzo, and Sonia Rykiel run the stylistic gamut from elegant to casual, serviceable to eye-awakening, sober to overtly decorative. A born innovator, Steiger first set trends by using fluorescent leather, transparent plastic, and exaggerated detailing.

» Casual and comfort

Everyday footwear

Fun, high-fashion shoes that stand up to special occasions often upstage the prosaic footwear we rely on every day of the week but that doesn't have to be the case. While most designers have yet to invent a high-heeled shoe that's tolerably comfortable day in day out, plenty of designers have devoted their careers to creating admirably smart, serviceable shoes that can be worn happily in comfort for long stretches of time.

Chanel pump

In 1957 Coco Chanel bucked the stiletto heel trend and, in collaboration with bespoke shoemaker Raymond Massaro, designed a clever, low-heeled beige pump with a black toecap. When paired with beige stockings, the high cut of the upper optically slimmed the foot and extended the line of the leg while the black patent toecap foreshortened the length of the foot. Since its creation, the basic style in countless incarnations has been a staple of every Chanel collection, although the staggeringly high fetish version Karl Lagerfeld showed in the 1990s might have caused Chanel to turn in her grave.

Casual

These days casual shoes—whether flat or high heeled—that are intended to be wearable all day are available in a broad range of styles. They tend to be highly functional shoes that are presentable enough for us to wear at the office but are also stylistically flexible to double up on weekends.

Bernardo

119 Mercer Street, #2S, New York, USA

Tel: 1 800 867 5054, www.bernardofootwear.com

Architect, author, structural engineer, and social commentator Bernard Rudofsky designed the inaugural collection of Bernardo sandals after they appeared in a 1944 exhibition of his work at New York's Museum of Modern Art. Rudofsky believed that most encased and heeled shoes deformed a woman's anatomy, so he based his line on monks' and gladiators' open sandals, which duplicated a barefoot experience. He collaborated with legendary fashion designers Emilio Pucci and Elsa Schiaparelli and in his day was cited as the instigator of a sandal revolution.

Since 2001, Dennis and Lynne Comeau, who formerly created footwear for Prada and Dolce & Gabanna, have been Bernardo's creative directors. As well as including their own designs, they are currently reissuing examples of Rudofsky's timeless, iconic flats.

Cindy Glass

Nakhle Bldg, Selim Bustros St, Achrafieh, Beirut

Tel: +961 (0)1 32 02 60, www.cindyglass.net

A Cindy Glass embroidered suede boot

EXPERT *Essential* Laya Rahman, a Franco-Lebanese designer who studied at Parsons School of Design in New York, was a filmmaker and photographer before she turned her hand to shoes. Since 2005 she has produced fun-loving, medium- to high-heeled boots and shoes in small quantities in Beirut, and she opened her Parisian store in 2007. Her tartan Mary Janes have heels and a wide band of elastic across the arch; the sides of her stilettos feature tattoos of pinup girls and hearts; her wide, Russian, vinyl boots are covered with miniature dots and her knitted sock boots sit squarely on towering wooden platforms.

Dr. Martens

17–19 Neal Street, Covent Garden, London, UK

Tel: +44 (0)20 7240 7555, www.drmartens.com

In 1945, Doctor Klaus Martens modified DMs or Docs (the familiar names for aficionados of this classic brand) from a standard issue army boot so that it supported an injured ankle. It went into production a few years later and then a British manufacturer bought the patent rights to the UK. He anglicized the name, refined the fit, added the yellow stitching, and trademarked the sole before its 1960 launch. That 1460 style, eight eyelet in an oxblood color became the uniform of mailmen and factory workers until it was appropriated by various disenfranchised youth movements throughout the 1970s and 1980s, when it became decidedly unisex. Production moved to China, but since 2007 it has returned to the UK. The functional Elevate collection attracts women who value its raised, durable wedge soles and light, Oxford uppers.

Fratelli Rossetti

Via Cesare Cantù 24, Parabiago, Milan, Italy

Tel: +39 03 31 552226, www.fratellirossetti.com

Diego, Dario, and Luca Rossetti now run the company their father established in 1953, producing basic lace-up sports shoes in a small village near Milan. Artisan craftsmen use top-grade leathers and follow upward of 150 steps to produce each pair of their sneakers, wedged sandals, and loafers. The company takes pride in preserving the top quality/reasonable price ratio they've spent years achieving. Los Angeles designer George Esquivel's recent tweak of the line rendered a feminized man's Oxford cut from buttery, white leather with perforated flowers, which is meant to be worn barefoot, without laces.

Irregular Choice Essential

38 Bond Street, Brighton, UK

Tel: +44 (0)1273 777 120,
www.irregularchoice.com

EXPERT *Essential* Based in Brighton, the passion for footwear he inherited from his father drives Dan Sullivan to design wild and wonderful Asia-produced shoes that reflect his "recapture the freedom that eloped with your youth" motto. Bursting with attitude, his pumps, flats, and boots are as streetwise as they are sweet and exude a Minnie Mouse, cartoon-like vibe. A pump may sport an overtly jagged, Brancusi heel, graphic stitching, fake astrakhan, a seriously floppy bow, or white leather wings. If they could speak, Sullivan reckons his collections would say, "I'm sparkling. Won't someone take me dancing?"

Irregular Choice: Abigail's Party multicheckered brogue

Jaime Mascaro

Calle Poife, 0 S/N, Ferreries, Menorca, Spain

Tel: +34 971 374 500, www.mascaro.com

Established more than a century ago in Menorca, Jaime Mascaro is currently in the hands of the family's third generation. Height, peep toes, and bling are key elements of Ursula Mascaro's line of affordable leather boots, strappy sandals, and slingbacks (and her husband David Bell heads Pretty Ballerina). Radically cute and low vamped, the flat slippers are cut from patent leather, suede, animal prints, or metallic leathers and adorned with bows, sparkles, lip outlines, locks and keys, or Swarovski crystals. The fold-up versions rank as THE handbag accessory women pull out when their feet need a vacation from their stilettos.

Kenneth Cole

610 Fifth Avenue, New York, USA

Tel: 212 373 5800, www.kennethcole.com

Born in Brooklyn in 1954, Cole and his father turned the fortunes of the family's shoe manufacturing company, El Greco, around by buying a Candie slide —an Italian slip on with a wooden sole and tapered high heel. Cole set up his own label in 1982 and became known for his streetwise line of chunky-soled, predominantly black shoes as well as his clever marketing, where positive political slogans urge social activism. His reasonably priced line is made in China and he has a no fur policy.

Stephane Kelian

30, rue Troyon, Sèvres, France

Tel: +33 2 41 58 94 13, www.stephane-kelian.com

Founded in Bourg-de-Peage by brothers Georges and Gerard Keloglanian in 1960, the company changed its name to Stephane Kelian in 1974 when the third brother, Stephane, joined. A traditional craft evolved into high fashion when they debuted a women's collection of mid-heel pumps with uppers that were formed by braiding leather directly onto the lasts. In the 1980s they collaborated with Maud Frizon, Claude Montana, Issey Miyake, and Jean Paul Gaultier. The Royer Group, which also owns Patrick Cox and Charles Jourdan, bought the company in 2007 and moved their production to Spain, but braiding is still Stephan Kelian's trademark material and the heels are still sensible. Recent collections have evoked the elegance of the 1940s.

Tashkent By Cheyenne

20 East 1st St, New York, USA

Tel: 212 691 0281, www.tashkentnyc.com

Women who collect Tashkent boots characterize them as the perfect vehicle for running around town and arriving looking pulled together and feeling sexy. Designer Cheyenne Morris majored in sculpture and cobbled her first pair of shoes at the age of 19. She has collaborated with clothing designers like Philip Lim and all her designs are handcrafted in Italy using traditional production methods.

Morris achieves a balance of femininity and function with sumptuous skins, putty-colored suedes, washed calf leathers, and metallic linens in silhouettes that run the gamut from slouched over-the-knee boots to eminently practical flat equestrian boots with hand-knitted shafts that expand to fit any and all legs.

The Zindane Peep-toe Heel by Tashkent

Her heeled ankle boot/sandal hybrid with its cutout reveals, metal buckles, and floppy, suede ties might have walked straight out of Carrie Bradshaw's closet.

Tods

Galleria Vittorio Emanuele II, Milan, Italy

Tel: +39 02 877 997, www.tods.com

Dorino Della Valle founded this Italian leather goods firm in the 1920s and his son, Diego, used technical innovation and marketing to bring the label into its current prominence. Beside Tods, the company also owns Roger Vivier, which has the acclaimed Bruno Frisoni as its current creative director. Tods' signature laced moccasin/driving shoes are classic and perennially fashionable. Thanks to a foam-backed leather interior and a slip-resistant layer of rubber bullets their flexible soles are super comfortable. As well as basic, buttery black, they come in an array of colors and materials from lime-green suede to red patent to silver lamé.

TOMS

3025 Olympic Boulevard, Santa Monica, CA, USA

Tel: 310 566 3170, www.toms.com

Whenever TOMS sells a pair of shoes it donates a pair to a needy child. Entrepreneur Blake Mycoskie originated this Los Angeles-based, philanthropic brand in 2006, after a number of barefooted children in Argentina motivated him to devise a One for One movement that, to date, has distributed over a million pairs of shoes to children in more than 20 countries. Predominantly

In the details

Genuine Italian vegetable-
tanned sole leather

» Cuoio vero Italiano

When *Cuoio Vero Italiano* is inscribed on the sole of
a shoe it simply means the sole is made of genuine
Italian leather, but the average shoe buyer
understandably misinterprets the label and assumes
that the entire shoe is leather.

When a *Fatto in Italia* sticker appears inside a shoe
or on its box there's an inherent implication that the
entire shoe was made in Italy when, in fact,
regulation only requires two out of five construction
stages to have occurred there. Similarly, a shoe
assembled in China, India, or Malaysia that's
subsequently shipped to Italy for the application of a
decorative buckle may also qualify for the label.

No set definition of both terms exists and the
European Commission is loathe to introduce one in
case it hampers free trade. Nevertheless the *Fatto in
Italia* assignation is still synonymous with luxury and
conjures up images of skilled craftsmen and artisans
producing finely crafted shoes that stem from age-
old, hands-on techniques.

Opposite: Shoes being sewn by hand

soft-soled, TOMS' serviceable styles are produced in Ethiopia, China, and Argentina and many take their cue from flat, canvas, fishermen's espadrilles, ballet flats, or denim desert boots. Crocheted flats have a utilitarian feel, and even the sequined, wedged pumps feel casual.

Tuccia Di Capri

1630 Pennsylvania Avenue, Miami Beach, USA

Tel: 305 534 5865, www.tucciadicapri.com

A love and respect for traditional, Italian sandal-making led former models Terri Coleman and Tove Nord to apprentice themselves to one of the last remaining cobblers on the isle of Capri and subsequently open their chic, white, Tuccia Di Capri salon. In the heart of Miami Beach they now fit, customize, and construct thongs and gladiators for women with shoe sizes between 4 and 12.

They source their vibrantly colored artisanal leathers, antique appliqués, metal buckles, and Swarovski crystals from Naples, Salerno, and Casandrino and turn them into classic, groovy sandals while their clients sip champagne. They maintain their signature look by offering a small portfolio of options—either a toe-ring or T-strap upper—and one of three classic wedge, flat, or kitten heel soles that they contour precisely to the customer's feet. The completed one-of-a-kind design is ready within an hour.

United Nude Essential

13 Floral Street, Covent Garden, London, UK

Tel: +44 (0)207 240 7106, www.unitednude.com

EXPERT *Essential* In 2003, Dutch architect Rem D. Koolhaas teamed up with Galahad Clark, a seventh-generation member of the Clark's shoemaking dynasty, to form United Nude. Koolhaas had already designed his Mobius, an innovative shoe whose upper is attached to a wide leather band that forms the heel and footbed.

The company now has several other miniature architectural structures in its line. The steel, cantilevered heel on the Eamz pump pays homage to a chair developed by the mid-20th century furniture designer, Charles Eames; slim stripes swirl across the heel and elasticized upper, forming a quasi belt around their snazzy Fold bootee. The conceptual shoes they concocted with Dutch fashion designer, Iris van Herpen, experiment with rapid prototyping and carbon fiber, and their curved, 6-inch heels are both futuristic and gravity defying.

United Nude's multicolored stripe Fold Hi bootee

Comfort

While many women are still waiting for a high-heeled shoe that's tolerably comfortable day in, day out, certain brands and designers have spent their careers creating shoes that offer strong degrees of comfort to women who need to wear shoes that offer extra support or width, but don't want to compromise on the beauty of the product.

Arche

237 rue du Faubourg St Honoré, Paris, France

Tel: +33 (0)1 42 27 88 46, www.arche-shoes.com

Founded in 1968 by Pierre Robert Helaine, Arche's casual boots, slip-ons, and sandals are quintessentially French. Characteristically plain and undecorated, they are designed in Paris and assembled by artisans in the Chateau region. Their breathable European and Nubuck leathers are water- and scratch-resistant and their latex cushioning is long lasting, flexible, and shock absorbing. The line's vast palette of vibrant, jewel-toned colors takes its cue from runway fashion, and traditional tanning keeps it dye fast. Helaine's philosophy still reflects the company's philosophy: "If you can't think, walk. If you are thinking too much, walk. If you are thinking bad thoughts, keep on walking."

Belgian Shoes

110 East 55th Street, New York, USA

Tel: 212 755 7372, www.belgianshoes.com

EXPERT *Essential* A hybrid slipper/moccasin, Belgian Shoes has had a cult following ever since Henri Bendel originated the label in the 1940s. These flat, soft-soled loafers epitomize the stylishly casual lifestyle of the privileged set that spends weekends in the Hamptons or retires to Palm Beach. Their comfort is tied to

093

The classic Belgian Shoes loafer, with contrast piping

a simple construction—they are sewn and then turned inside out—and they come in one classic style. Plain or with contrasting piping, crested or monogrammed; they can be special ordered by mail. They come in every color imaginable and in a host of fabrics that includes plush velvet, lizard, and two-toned linen. Some of their more popular styles are on a two-year back order.

Belstaff

12–13 Conduit Street, London, UK

Tel: +44 (0)207 495 5897, www.belstaff.com

Harry Grosberg founded Belstaff in the Midlands, UK, in 1924 to make waterproof garments for men and women from breathable Egyptian waxed cotton.

The brand is now an Italian company headed by Manuele and Michele Malenotti. Their shoe division, set up in 2002, produces a line of classic, slim-shafted boots from calf's leather that are fast becoming as iconic as the company's motorcycle jacket. Apart from antiqued buckles and channeled stitching the boots are plain and unadorned except for their heeled Victorian boots, which feature 30 eyelets and extensive brogueing.

Birkenstock

Rheinstraße 2–4, Vettelschoß, Germany

Tel: +49 (0)26 45 942 100, www.birkenstock.de

Made from renewable cork, the supremely supportive footbed of Birkenstock's flat sandals and clogs relaxes the foot's muscles and follows its natural contours, while a deep heel cup stabilizes the body in a perfect balance and absorbs shock. A roomy fit allows toes to wiggle freely, and each size comes in either a narrow or regular width.

The company uses solvent-free glue and non-corrosive buckles, and it also offers repairs and caters to customers who have very wide or different sized feet. After 200 years the Birkenstock family still owns the company and still manufactures in Germany. In recent years the brand lost its devoutly granola image, when it briefly utilized Popsicle-colored suede and gold and silver lamés—and even though the collection is now back to basics, Birkenstock will customise colors and materials on request.

Blundstone

88 Gormanston Road, Moonah, Tasmania,
Australia

Tel: +61 (0)3 6271 2222, www.blundstone.com

John and Eliza Blundstone developed the firm in
1870 in Tasmania to develop footwear that catered to
the harsh Australian outback. From the beginning,
the sole of every Blundstone shoe or boot had a
revolutionary shock-protection system that reduced
fatigue and orthopedic problems in the lower back,
legs, and feet. Recent tests produced evidence that
their soles reduce about one-third of normal shock
transmitted to the leg at a brisk walking pace and
there's even an additional copyrighted pad in the
heel strike zone for extra shock protection. Their
Blunnies (slip-on ankle boots with elasticized sides
and oversized tabs) are their signature, unisex style.
Even though most of their production has moved to
Thailand and India, they are still committed to a
minimum usage of raw materials, chemicals, and
fossil fuels.

Born

www.bornshoes.com

Since 1995 Born has cut their rugged-looking
sandals and clogs from supple leather and outfitted
them with shock-absorbing foam that ensures
absolute comfort. Most styles are offered in medium
and wide widths and all employ an Opanka
construction where the sock lining, upper, and
outsole are hand-sewn together in a single process
with heavily waxed, durable thread. Despite their

structural sturdiness, the shoes are lightweight and ideally make their wearer feel as if she is barefoot.

The Born Crown label carries more fashion forward, feminine mules and heeled sandals that use the same Opanka construction. Ballet flats come in plaid velvet, linen, paisley, adorned with a discrete bow and a decoratively embossed traction sole.

Camper

Sirena, 13, Inca, Spain

Tel: +34 971 501164, www.camper.com

Owned by a Majorcan family that has manufactured unisex footwear since 1877, Camper (meaning "peasant" in Catalan) was launched as a label in 1975. Quirky, retro sneakers have stitched stripes; asymmetrical Mary Janes are vividly color-blocked, while other styles have messages or poems inscribed on their soles. All their collections are edgy, alternative, graphic, chic, and eminently functional and they consider themselves outside the fashion industry. The company's motto, "walk don't run" appeals to a number of product and furniture designers like Hella Jongerius, Jasper Morrison, and the Bourellec Brothers, who have collaborated on shoes and appreciate the firm's attention to detail.

Castañer

Carrer del Mestre Nicolau, 23, Barcelona, Spain

Tel: +34 934 142428, www.castaner.com

Founded in 1927 by Luis Castañer and Tomas Serra in an espadrille workshop, the company peaked in 1936 during the Spanish Civil War when uniforms

Words from the wise

Karen Williamson, Founder and CEO of barefoottess.com

» Large sizes

In the 1900s, the average woman's shoe size was a US 5 (see page 24 for international sizes); by the mid 1900s it had increased to 7 and it's currently 9. The shoe industry, however, is behind the times, so if you have large feet it's incredibly frustrating. You're constantly teased with media stories about fabulous styles that aren't available to you. Eventually the shoe industry will catch up, but when it does, prepare for small sizes to become a rarity.

If you wear tiny shoes, toe cleavage is cute but that's not the case with a size 12 or 13 and moccasin-type, non-form fitting vamps in those sizes are best avoided. In large sizes plain vamps can look orthopedic so choose detailing—stitching, appliqués, buckles, or belts—that lessens and feminizes that bulk. The proportions of most boots flatter women who wear large sizes—cowboys with roomy shafts, wellies, scrunchy bootees that fold down, and over-the-knees boots all look fabulous. They are the one style that most small women simply can't pull off.

for soldiers fighting at the front included espadrilles. In the mid-1960s, after Yves Saint Laurent ordered a high-heeled espadrille for his runway, the company's profile went from casual country to city chic. Castañer now makes lighthearted boots, shoes, and sandals with wedges wrapped in hemp rope, woven straw, rattan, wicker, seersucker, or patent leather.

Chie Mihara

Calle lepanto 20-altos, Elda-Alicante, Spain

Tel: +34 9669 80415, www.chiemihara.com

EXPERT *Essential* Born in Brazil, Mihara studied fashion in Japan and New York, where she interned in a store that sells orthopedic footwear. She designed for Sam & Libby and then moved to Spain, where she currently lives and manufactures, to create shoes for Charles Jourdan. The line she established in 2001 is feminine, nostalgic, and smart. Dressmaking references abound—petal detailing covers a heel; ruched straps crisscross a vamp; topstitching exaggerates a T-strap. She permanently has an eye on comfort, so she favors open toes; her 4-inch-high ankles boots have a concealed 1-inch platform; her ankle straps have wide adjustments and her enclosed shoes have substantial leather insoles.

Osmo suede sandal with adjustable buckle, by Chie Mihara

Cole Haan

673 No. Michigan Ave, Chicago, Illinois, USA

Tel: 1 800 695 8945, www.colehaan.com

Started by Trafton Cole and Eddie Haan in Chicago
in 1928, the company first focused on men's penny
loafers and saddle shoes, before venturing into
women's shoes in 1979, and subsequently selling
unisex driving shoes. Now owned by Nike, sneaker
technology infuses comfort into the brand's stylistically
conservative, utilitarian flats and mid-heeled pumps,
boots, and ankle-strapped sandals. Every so often a
classic style appears rejuvenated in a jaw dropping,
vivid color, but the label rarely pushes the stylistic
envelope, which reassures a devoted fan base that
places great value on simple, comfortable silhouettes.

Dansko

8 Federal Road, West Grove PA, USA

Tel: 1 800 326 7564, www.dansko.com

Founded by Mandy Cabot and her husband Peter
Kjellerun in 1990, Dansko still prioritizes
comfortable shoes so the company's collections of
clogs, boots, flats, and sandals support and align the
toes, arch, and heel. Their clogs have roomy toe
boxes that promote circulation, a stress-reducing
rocker bottom, and superior arch support. The label
is particularly loved by nurses, chefs, and anyone
who has to stand up for long periods of time. The
company has a commitment to the environment so
it utilizes as many renewable resources as possible.

Ecco

16 Delta Dr, Londonderry, NH, USA

www.eccousa.com

Karl Toosbuy launched Ecco shoes in the 1970s in a small town on the west coast of Denmark and they became an instant hit. It's now ranked as one of the five largest producers of quality leather in the world. From the outset, Toosbuy favored comfort over conformity and, to this day, the line remains oblivious to fashion trends. All the styles are basic and sensible, and come in practical or subdued colors with an occasional foray into lime green or powder pink. They are still mostly produced by hand even though the company is also a world leader in direct injection technology. Designed in Denmark, the construction details are transferred electronically to Thailand, Indonesia, Slovakia, and China.

French Sole

985 Lexington Avenue, New York, USA

Tel: 212 737 2859, www.frenchsoleshoes.com

 Owned by Randy Ochart, French Sole is a tiny store on Manhattan's upper east side and it has carried a phenomenally large selection of ballet flats for the last 25 years. Culled from Spain, Italy, France, and Brazil, more than 500 styles come in a myriad of colors and materials. Tasseled, sequinned, toe-capped, pointy, striped, ruffled, perforated, crested, or plain—each style, from casual to conservative, fuses fashion with comfort as it molds to the wearer's foot. Ochart will outfit anyone, from ages 8 to 80, whether they crave the casual, cute, or conservative.

Frye

113 Spring Street, New York, USA

Tel: 212 226 3793,
www.thefryecompany.com

French Sole Leopard toe ballerinas

Founded in Marlboro, Massachusetts in 1863 by John A. Frye, a shoemaker from England, the Frye Company supplied shoes to soldiers on both sides in the Civil War, and for Teddy Roosevelt and his Rough Riders in the Spanish-American war.

New England families wore Frye boots as they pioneered across the country and, today, the classic Harness boot with its high-belted vamp is an iconic element in America's history of clothing. The women's range of heeled Oxfords, nail-head trimmed clogs, and antiqued penny loafers are all constructed from full-grain leathers that are tanned with natural oils and hang-dried for a crunch effect. It takes 190 steps to make one pair of Frye boots.

Hunter

36 Melville Street, Edinburgh, Scotland, UK

Tel: +44 (0)1312 403 672, www.hunter-boot.com

Hunters were originally designed at the beginning of the 19th century for men who preferred to wear trousers rather than breeches. The first Duke of Wellington subsequently instructed his shoemaker to modify the boots, and the result was a soft, calfskin, leather boot with its trim removed. The boots, nicknamed Wellies, caught on. An American entrepreneur, Henry Lee Norris, set up shop with his master bootmaker in Scotland in 1856 and duplicated the boots in rubber. After many incarnations the Green Hunter emerged in 1958 and over the course of 50 years has become a unisex favorite. The leg of the Royal Hunter is luxuriously lined with soft leather.

John Fluevog

65 Water Street, Vancouver, BC, Canada

Tel: 604 688 6228, www.fluevog.com

In 1970, Fluevog and his then partner, Peter Fox, opened an old warehouse full of vintage, dead-stock footwear. In the 1980s, after their partnership dissolved, Fluevog set up shops throughout the States selling affordable designs that had a pronounced vintage feel. Solidly constructed in places as varied as Portugal and Peru, their limited palette of blacks and browns and graphic brogue stitching attracted punks, Goths, and rockabillies who looked upon Fluevog's unisex lace-up boots and brothel creepers as a groovy alternative to their beloved Dr. Martens (see page 82). Fluevog currently lives in Vancouver and still produces characterful shoes—pink, open-toed Oxfords with a modified Louis heel; skinny-heeled T-straps with scalloped edging; and sartorial knee boots with oversized eyelets and wide ribbon ties.

K. Jacques

32 ZA Saint Claude, Route des Plages, Saint-Tropez, France

Tel: +33 49 49 74 150, www.kjacques.fr

The K. Jacques line of sandals began life in 1933 in a small workshop in Saint-Tropez, where Jacques Keklikian and his wife cobbled custom sandals for tourists, and before long the style epitomized the French Riviera. Over time, the unassuming gladiator sandals with ankle straps or simple toe straps and unisex Roman sandals appeared at Jean-Charles Castelbajac and Karl Lagerfeld fashion shows. The current line—flat or heeled cork wedges, straps in calfskin, alligator, sharkskin, or colorful metallic—is intended for day and evening wear.

K. Jacques Agopos sandal

Lucchese

40 Walter Jones Blvd, El Paso, Texas, USA

www.lucchese.com

In 1880, Sam Lucchese and his brothers came to the US and, three years, later started their Lucchese Boot Company. In 1960, the founder's grandson and namesake took over the business and decided to fashion a boot with unrivaled comfort. The boots are made in El Paso on twisted cone lasts that simulate the turn of the foot as it slips inside a boot. As much attention is paid to the proportional dimension of the instep, ball, and heel height as it is to the use of fine-grade leathers and meticulous decorative stitching.

Maloles Antignac

62, rue Tiquetonne, Paris, France

Tel: +33 (0)1 42 96 86 51, www.maloles.com

Maloles Antignac studied at the Institute Français de la Mode, and in 2004, launched a shoe brand that centered around two styles of ballet slippers. From a design point of view they were upside down, because they featured the pleated leather that normally appears on a ballet slipper's under sole on their vamps. In subsequent collections she added pumps, boots, and Oxfords but the ballets are still thought of as her signature style. Coquettish, striped, and colorful, with bows and keyholes worked into their uppers, they are constructed in Spain from Italian leathers.

Minnetonka Moccasin

1113 East Hennepin Avenue, Minneapolis, USA

Tel: 612 331 8493,
www.minnetonkamoccasin.com

Based on authentic American Indian footwear, this company has been run by three generations of the same family for more than 60 years. Price worthy, comfortable, and durable, a range of skins—glove tanned leather, deerskin, sheepskin, and moose hide—is fashioned into plain or beaded moccasins and fringed ankle- and calf-high boots.

Repetto

30, avenue de Messine, Paris, France

Tel: + 33 (0)1 44 71 83 00, www.repetto.com

Rose Repetto created her first pair of ballet shoes for her choreographer son Roland Petit in a tiny Parisian workshop in 1956, and went on to supply the world's greatest dancers. The company is still revered for its pointe and jazz shoes but their line extends to street-wearable flats that are tie-dyed or encrusted with sequins or polka dots, as well as high-heeled Oxfords with generous toecaps.

Rieker

www.riekerfootwear.co.uk

Markus Rieker opened his first factory near the German Black Forest in 1874 and since its inception the company has seen itself as an antistress brand bent on producing footwear that brings a sense of well-being to its wearers. Their tapered knee-high boots, utilitarian sandals, suede slip-ons, and stylish court shoes are all lightweight, flexible, shock absorbing, and roomy, with cushiony soles and walkable heels. Rieker currently ranks as one of the largest shoe enterprises in Europe and it takes 50 steps to produce each shoe.

Rosa Mosa

Mollardgasse 85A/3/125+126, Vienna, Austria

Tel: +43 1 941 03 19, www.rosamosa.com

Simone Springer, a graduate of the Academy of Fine Arts in Vienna, and Yuji Mizobuchi, a former student of Buddhist philosophy in Kyoto, teamed up while studying footwear design Cordwainers in London. The series of carved, wooden sandals they created together immediately won awards. They studied with a bespoke shoemaker in Brighton and then moved to Vienna to launch their Rosa Mosa label. Included in a recent collection produced in Eastern Europe, there is an innocent-looking Mary Jane; a heeled sandal whose vamp has a braided upper inspired by a rag-weaving technique; a bootee with a kilim shaft; and innovative clogs with polyurethane soles that flex.

Terra Plana

64 Neal Street, Covent Garden, London, UK

Tel: +44 (0)1458 449 069, www.vivobarefoot.com

In 1998 Lance Clark took over Terra Firma, a company founded by Charles Bergmans in the early 1990s. Presently under the leadership of Clark's son, Galahad, the firm produces eco-friendly, pastel sneakers and retro-looking pumps from chrome-free leather, where recast foam footbeds match with 90 percent latex soles. A second brand, Vivo Barefoot, features sneakers and boots with ultra-thin Kevlar soles that simulate walking without shoes and the funky side-buttoned Worn Again sneakers, which are made from recycled parachutes and patchwork tweed jackets.

Thierry Rabotin

Via dell'Industria, 38–40/C, Busto Garolfo, Milan, Italy

Tel: +39 0331 495 007, www.thierryrabotin.com

Thierry Rabotin was born in the 1950s in a small west-central village in France and designed women's wear until 1978, when he switched his focus to footwear. His eminently comfortable signature chaussons have a sacchetto construction, where a leather, sack-like shape is sewn directly onto the edge of the upper. The shoe has no rigid parts or metal shank so it is flexible, lightweight, and ventilated, thanks to a breathable layer between the upper and lining. Rabotin makes his simple peep-toed sandals from glove-like nappa and patent leathers, and he never builds heels higher than 3 inches. Sequins and rhinestones are sparingly used as embellishments and colors are pale and natural, with a favored palette that spans from pearl gray to sooty black.

UGG

The Grove, 189 The Grove Drive #F72, Los Angeles, CA, USA

Tel: 323 275 1227, www.uggaustralia.com

EXPERT Essential In the late 1960s surfers on beaches of Byron Bay Australia kept their feet warm in between sessions with homemade "footies" constructed from local sheepskin and a completely flat sole. In 1978, Brian Smith took the idea to the beaches of southern California and by the mid 1980s the trend cropped up in ski lodges and the line expanded to clogs, slippers, sneakers, and wedges.

Blush Classic Tall
Romantic Flower UGG boot

Their signature-grade, twin-face sheepskin is dense, soft, and malleable, and comes in earthy colors as well as powder pink and baby blue. Variations on a theme are the allover sequin boot and the Cardy Ugg that's wrapped in a knitted, buttoned sleeve.

Wicked Hemp

PO Box 388, Alton, NH 03809, USA

www.wickedhemp.com

Wicked Hemp has a mandate to reduce their company's carbon footprint, so they only use eco- and animal-friendly components in all their hiking boots. Hemp, a rapidly renewable fiber, requires no pesticides and fertilizers to grow, and is resistant to mold, mildew, salt, and water, which makes their sneakers particularly popular with chefs. Tree pulp harvested from hemlocks, spruce, and pines is basket-woven into uppers, while natural rubber constitutes their vegan-friendly soles.

Vegan materials

Producers of vegan shoes, especially Stella McCartney's well-established, fashion-forward line, avoid using all animal skins in their designs. Instead they use a range of alternative materials, including faux leather, Perspex, cork, satin, and blended fibers.

» Possess

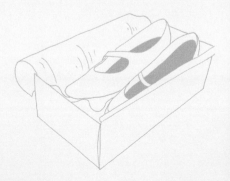

Buying shoes online

The experience of trying on a pair of shoes in an actual store with the aid of a friend or a knowledgeable salesperson is invaluable. However, most retailers and individual designers now own e-commerce sites, and the many options of aggregate websites that curate their inventory from a host of manufacturers are more popular and dependable than ever.

Despite not being able to try the shoe on, nothing beats the the 24/7 convenience, price comparison possibilities, and enormous range of styles and brands offered on the Internet. Also, unlike actual stores, stock offered online isn't dictated by season.

When shopping on these sites it helps if you are already familiar with each brand's unique method of sizing and fabrication. Each site has its own viewpoint, distinct voice, and unique set of terms, but most offer liberal return policies, a very quick turn around and, depending on your location, free or flat-rate shipping.

» The size trap

The obvious disadvantage to overcome when buying shoes online is not knowing the exact fit. Upscale shoe stores will generally have a certified fit specialist on staff who can measure your foot on a Brannick device to assess its girth and character. They can tell you whether you have high arches, longer than average toes, wide insteps, slim ankles, or muscular calves and suggest the types of shoes that flatter your attributes. When you buy online you need all this knowledge at hand. This information is accessible on every site but it may be spread between a blog, chart, self-measuring video, or live chat room.

There is no standardization for shoe sizes and one designer's idea of "wide" might be "extra wide" to another designer, or "narrow" to one designer might involve you dropping a size as far as another designer is concerned. If you have a favorite brand, stick with it where possible, because the sizing is a known entity.

Buying sneakers online is relatively simple and most of us can buy shoes based on a single measurement but boot shopping requires three measurements—foot size, calf circumference, and lower-leg length, measured from your heel base to knee joint, and which corresponds to the boot's shaft.

» **Delivery and exchanges**
If a shoe is already backordered it may take weeks to arrive, otherwise purchases can be delivered immediately. Many sites offer free shipping, otherwise the mailing cost will be added as you check out. Be aware that international shipping can add a considerable amount to your order. Most sites offer an easy return/exchange policy and some even offer free shipping rates on returns, but every site is unique, so make sure you read their terms before you make your purchase.

When the shoes arrive, try them on with the tights or socks you plan to wear with them and return them as soon as possible if they are not right.

111

Online shopping is an incredible resource for hard-to-find, specialist sizes and widths and most sites break their search options down into styles, heel heights, colors, widths, and even materials so that it is quick and easy to find what you're looking for.

» Where to buy

Many of the designers in the earlier chapters have websites from which you can purchase their shoes. The following list is a selection of websites that stock collections from a variety of different designers and brands.

Brandos

www.brandos.com

Brandos, a Swedish-based company, operates internationally in eight countries and is considered to be northern Europe's largest online shoe store, with thousands of styles and a particularly impressive selection of bridal shoes. Brands include Michael Kors, Hush Puppies, Vans, Calvin Klein, Esprit, Charles David, and many more.

Luisaviaroma

www.luisaviaroma.com

Based in Florence, this site carries a heavily edited portfolio of luxury designer shoes. Brands include Balmain, Fendi, Jil Sander, Jimmy Choo, Lanvin, Marc Jacobs, Pierre Hardy, Rick Owens, and many more. They also have an edgy, in-the-know blog with live feeds to the runway shows during the collections.

OnlineShoes
www.onlineshoes.com

Originated from a neighborhood store in Seattle, Washington, this site specializes in comfort shoes with brands including Rieker, Liz Claibourne, Vivo Barefoot, Ugg, Born, Enzo Angioloni, Merrill, New Balance, and much more. Additionally, if you discover a lower price elsewhere they will match it. They have a multiple-view option that shows shoes from a variety of angles.

Jewelry for the feet

Bejeweled shoes always have been, and always will be, the most feminine of shoes. They simulate the experience of stepping into a work of art. Historically women of all cultures have enjoyed adorning their feet for their own pleasure as a part of their beautifying routine. Jewelers and cobblers worked side by side in the bazaars of ancient Egypt; Cleopatra was renowned for wearing lavishly jeweled sandals with patterned soles; glittering shoes worn by 17th-century European courtiers featured eye-popping stones; and in the 18th century, emeralds were often sewn into a heel's back seam in a *venez y voir* trend. In many cultures where shoes are customarily removed when indoors, women routinely embellish their naked feet with ankle bracelets and toe rings.

The Outnet

www.outnet.com

Aimed at "savvy fashionistas" who love a bargain, this discounted affiliate of net-a-porter.com carries designer fashion and shoes from recent seasons at up to 70 percent off retail. The site guarantees the authenticity of more than 200 brands including Balmain, Christian Louboutin, Calvin Klein, and Valentino. They routinely offer flash sales but, as is the case with any outlet, availability of sizes and stock can be limited and short-lived.

Pavers

www.pavers.co.uk

An informative blog and sales site that focuses on trainers, boots, and comfort footwear. Brands include Skechers, New Balance, Vivo Barefoot, Trimsole, Fly Flots, and more. They carry an impressive range of widths from D to EEEE.

Shoebuy

www.shoebuy.com

A Boston-based site that sells over 1,200 brands including Sorel, Bruno Magli, Joan & David, Mephisto, Naturalizer, Nina, and more. They have a niche market for hard-to-find sizes and some styles ship the same day. There's a strong charitable component to the business and a large sale site with up to 65 percent reductions. They offer Facebook Credits with each purchase.

Shoes of Prey

www.shoesofprey.com

Based in Australia, and launched in 2009 by Michael and Jody Fox, this site utilizes a fun, interactive, 360-degree view tool that enables online customers to design their own shoes and ankle boots from 12 generic styles, and then go on to customize the backs, toes, heels, materials, and colors. Their shoes are offered in a wide range of sizes, from a US 2 to 14 (see page 24 for international measurements). Built by artisans, they ship internationally within five weeks and can be returned for any reason. They also make pairs of shoes for women whose feet are different sizes.

Zappos.com

www.zappos.com

Based in Nevada and owned by Amazon.com, Zappos, including the online boutique Zappos Couture, carry upward of 50,000 varieties of shoes and is considered to be the largest online shoe store in the world. Brands include Guess, Robert Clergerie, Fitzwell, Kork-Ease, Juicy Couture, Kate Spade, Badgley Mischka, and many more. They pride themselves on the broad range of Vegan shoes and their highly trained sales support team is reportedly the best in the business.

Vintage shoes

Sweet nostalgia is one of the most attractive aspects of vintage shoes, and the relative affordability of a second-hand Ferragamo or Gucci appeals strongly to any women who may not be able to afford them new. The thrill of the hunt also plays a part, especially when an obscure or legendary label shows up in a charity shop at a giveaway price. Exotic reptilian leathers that are no longer politically correct to manufacture or extraordinarily expensive can be acquired for a manageable amount. Also, when you find a used shoe you love in your size the chances are slim that you'll encounter anyone else wearing a duplicate pair and that warrants as the biggest payoff for many women.

If you plan to wear the shoes, buy them in person, because online sellers tend to offer up bare-bones descriptions and unless they are "unworn vintage stock" the shoes will have already molded themselves to someone else's foot and so their compatibility to your foot is anyone's guess.

If you do buy online, ask for the shoe's measurements as well as its printed size—pay particular attention to width and be prepared to write it off as a gamble purchase if it's a "must have" and the seller doesn't have a returns policy. A seller's "mint condition" description is subjective and some (but not all) of a shoe's parts are easily upgraded or replaced at a price: a deteriorated lining, for example, can be removed but it is not repairable.

Words from the wise

Cheyenne Morris Shoe designer
and collector

» Venturing out for vintage

If you fall in love with vintage shoes where the
leather is cracked or in a state of disrepair, it's sad to
say but no amount of polishing and repairing can
resuscitate them. If they're still wearable, you can
enjoy breathing new life into them but also think
about displaying them and appreciating them as
architectural works of art.

When looking for vintage shoes, the best sources
are vintage clothing stores, eBay, and auctions, but if
you find yourself bidding against a curator or serious
collector, be prepared for steep prices.

Nowadays we wear a wide range of styles to express
all the aspects of our personality so an average closet
may contain everything from a Blahnik to a
Birkenstock, but footwear from the 1930s, '40s and
'50s illustrates how women conformed to society's
definition of a "lady" so they're like a photograph of
a bygone era, and they are wonderful collectors'
pieces to own.

Cleaning and protecting

It's important to take proper care of your shoes to make them last as long as possible, and knowing the proper cleaning care is essential so that you don't do more harm than good.

There are particular ways of cleaning different materials, so make sure you know what material you are treating before you start. One general guideline is that, no matter what material it is made from, never dry a wet pair of shoes in direct sunlight or with artificial heat.

The life of most materials can also be extended with regular home treatments of waterproofing spray. Bolster a wet upper with tissue paper rather than newspaper to prevent ink imprints on your feet the next time you wear your shoes. And don't forget to brush and clean a shoe's heel and mid sole.

» Leather

Clean a leather shoe by applying a liquid pH-neutral soap mixed in water to its entire surface. Spot-remove scratches with a light solution of water mixed with baking soda and then buff dry.

Salt picked up from street cleaning is very corrosive so remove traces of it with a rag soaked in a water/white vinegar solution then rinse it off with a dampened cloth and towel the shoe dry. After cleaning apply a cream conditioner.

>> Fabric

Use a special textile waterproofing spray for dress shoes with toile, linen, or brocade uppers. Wash general dirt away under running warm water with the aid of a very soft brush and remove dried dirt with a slightly harsher brush.

>> Synthetic

For plastic or neoprene uppers, use a polishing sponge impregnated with silicone, then lightly buff the surface with a damp cloth.

>> Lacquer

Light buffing with a cream polish removes scratches and scuffs from a patent leather shoe. Avoid any harsh chemicals that may dissolve the shoe's high-gloss, waterproofed surface.

>> Rubber

Generally speaking, Wellington boots and other rubber shoes should be cleaned with water followed by a cloth buffing. Spot-clean scratches with a nonabrasive kitchen cleanser.

>> Suede

Brush off any general dirt that may have accumulated on a napped surface once it is completely dry, then spot-clean it with a kneadable art eraser. Raise a flattened nap by scrubbing it with a clean toothbrush or a terry cloth towel, or hold it a few inches away from the spout of a steaming kettle then brush it lightly. Take a nail file to really stubborn stains, but beware of lightening the surface in the process.

» **White sneakers**
Soak the laces and clean the uppers in watered-down laundry detergent, then wipe with a clean cloth. Spot-clean the surface with dabs of whitening toothpaste brushed in a circular motion; once a stain

UNIQUE » RARE » LITTLE-KNOWN » **ULTIMATE EXPERT**

Pricy prized shoes In 2002 designer Stuart Weitzman established a tradition of providing an Oscar nominee with a pair of "million dollar shoes" for the duration of the awards ceremony. For the first pair he set 464 pear- and round-shaped Kuwait diamonds in platinum. In subsequent pairs he took inspiration from Marilyn Monroe's jewelry estate and incorporated ruby, sapphire, and diamond earrings once owned by Rita Hayworth in the design of sandals that had to be insured for $3 million. The two diamond rose buckles he affixed to his 2008 stilettos utilized 1,800 Kuwait diamonds that weighed 100 carats.

lifts, wash the entire area with a damp cloth to remove all the paste. A mix of baking soda and water works particularly well on canvas.

If you are running your sneakers through the washing machine, place them in a mesh bag first. Never put them in a dryer because the heat reacts with the shoe's adhesive and can weaken its seams.

» Silk

Uppers made from silk, or made using a satin weave, are very delicate so it is often best to use a professional cleaning service. If that isn't an option, slip your hand inside a nylon stocking and remove dirt with repeated wipes; spray the shoes with seltzer water or sponge them with a water and liquid handsoap solution. If the stains persist, you can dye the uppers a shade or two darker.

» Boots

All leather boots respond well when they are cleaned and conditioned with saddle soap—a waxy mix of lanolin, beeswax, glycerin, and neatsfoot oil. Use a squirt bottle to dilute the soap and work it into a lather while it's still in the tin. Distribute the lather over the boot, let it dry and then rub it smooth with a soft, absorbent cloth.

Shoe repairs

A repair process that involves dismantling a shoe entirely, or in parts, will be costly, so make sure to enlist a cobbler that is not only a reputable craftsman but one who also understands fashion trends and style nuances.

» Stretching

Shoe stretching is best handled at home and done gradually with the aid of a kit that includes a hardwood or plastic stretcher, spot-stretching implements, and permanent shoe-stretch spray. Soft leather uppers are the most pliable candidates, while patent and plastic rarely stretch successfully.

» Soles

Many women routinely have their new shoes resoled with rubber before they first wear them as a safety measure that also prolongs a shoe's life.

» Heels

Inserting heel grips, replacing heel tips, and leather heel covers are standard fare for most cobblers but building up a heel's height or replacing a heel's base requires a sensitivity to a shoe's overall architecture, as does straightening a wobbly heel, a process that often involves inserting a new shank. Repairs such as these should only be undertaken by a skilled cobbler who keeps a wide range of replacement heels in stock. Judge a cobbler's repertoire according to whether his standard bill of fare includes re-crafting cowboy boots and rejuvenating Birkenstocks—two

Words from the wise

Jim Rocco Owner of Jim's Shoe Repair

» Maintenance and alteration

If you treat them properly, well-made shoes will last for decades, especially if they're rotated and not worn every day. Assess the condition of your shoes every time you take them off and regularly nourish the leather with cream that's easily absorbed and lets the leather breathe—wax tends to build up layers unless it's completely removed and then the leather chokes and starts to crack.

If the fit of your shoe is not perfect, certain aspects can be altered by a good cobbler: comfort can be increased by inserting gel insoles, arch supports, and padding; if a boot cuts into your knee it can be shortened; one that is too wide can have the shaft taken in; if it's too tight a gusset can be inserted; and a shoe can be widened and stretched to an extent (although it cannot actually be made longer).

One thing that is very difficult is to lower the height of a dress shoe. The entire heel has to come off and if it's reduced by more than ¼-inch (5mm), the shoe's overall architecture is totally compromised.

tasks that require craftsmanship—and always ask to see their work before you entrust them with a favorite pair of shoes.

≫ Interiors

Do-it-yourself heel liners and cork footbeds increase a shoe's fit and comfort level, but nothing increases arch support like a customized orthotic that slips into most closed shoes and boots.

≫ Vamps

Patronize a cobbler who has a wide inventory of replacement buckles and who takes it in stride when an elastic gusset or ankle strap needs to be replaced.

Buckles

Shoe buckles can be symbols of power, nobility, gentility, or mere ostentation. Their popularity peaked in the mid 1600s when Louis XIV turned out his feet and pointed his toes while performing a ballet to show off his buckles (inadvertently laying the foundation for the five basic ballet positions). Buckles stayed at the height of fashion during the Restoration era, 1660–1700, but disappeared during the Revolution in the 1780s, and were replaced by utilitarian laces. According to fashion dictates jewelers have set them in marcasite or gems and they even japanned them black for mourning during La Belle Epoque.

Accessories

You'll find a number of different accessories are available to accompany your shoe collection. Many of these are made to help keep shoes in good condition, whether they maintain the shape, provide proper storage, or help you to put them on and then take them off.

» **Travel and storage**

Even when a travel bag or carrying case has an allotted space for shoes, individual felt bags with a drawstring are the best way to protect shoes when you travel. Use portable packages of baby wipes to remove excess dirt and dust from uppers and soles and even though plastic boot trees are lightweight, rolled up magazines do just the same trick.

» **Shoe trees**

Traditionally a shoe tree is a solid piece of aromatic, contoured wood, such as cedar, and it fits snugly inside a shoe to retain its shape, absorb odor, and wick away moisture. It's held in place with a screw device or a spring-activated rod. Plastic versions are designed for travel.

» **Shoe boxes**

True aficionados like to store their shoes in their original cardboard box, but nothing can beat the practicality and high-visibility factor of stackable, clear-plastic boxes that showcase their contents.

» Boot jack

A jack or boot pull is made of metal or wood. It has a U-shaped mouth and a leverage ledge that turns boot removal into an easy, one-step process.

» Boot hooks

Pairs of curved metal hooks with wooden handles are specifically designed to slip into the long loops located inside the tall, form-fitting shafts of equestrian boots. They hold the boot in place while the wearer slips them on.

» Shoe horn

A horn or shoespooner is a smooth, tongue-shaped tool that slips behind the heel and allows a person to glide their foot inside a shoe. Nowadays they are predominantly plastic, wood, or metal but collectable antique versions were formed from animal hoofs, horn, ivory, silver, shell, and bone. Long-handled versions remove the need for people to bend while putting on their shoes

» Boot shapers

Related to shoe trees, these plastic, spring-activated shapers mimic the contours and width of a boot's shaft and are designed to retain shape and encourage air to circulate.

» Shoe or boot stretchers

These wooden or plastic devices are designed to apply pressure to the inside of a shoe or boot, to expand its width. Some are spring loaded while others have adjustable plugs so the pressure can be customized to fit.

» Shoe racks

Closet organizers come in all shapes and sizes. Some metal-pronged racks spin, while others are made of canvas cubbies that can be velcroed to a closet's clothing bar. Others have a grid of pockets and are designed to hang over a closet door. Cloth allows leather to breathe and provides a degree of ventilation while clear plastic allows shoes to be easily seen at a glance.

» Padding

Slim, gel cushions act as shock absorbers and help minimize fatigue, pain, and stress on the ball of the foot, heel, and arch while they inject stability into every style of pump, sandal, flat, or heel. Contoured metatarsal pads decrease the pressure in the mid-foot and are particularly beneficial in sports shoes; forefoot pads prevent feet from shifting in sandals and open-toed shoes. TPE, or thermoplastic elastomers, mix plastic and rubber to form a cushioning material with open, moisture-repelling cells that let air flow freely and retain their shape over long-term use. They are sold in strips or pads with scalloped edges and adhere to a shoe's interior wall, bed, or strap. They reduce pressure from tight shoes or help large shoes fit more snugly as they prevent calluses and protect blisters.

When to wear

Shoes clearly play a significant role in most women's lives—the mere act of shopping for new shoes can be a mood-elevating pastime—but how prominent a role should a shoe play in the overall scheme of an outfit? There was a time when stylish women wore shoes that matched their handbags, but that's no longer the case outside of a parody of the Stepford Wives.

» The main event

Some women buy neutral shoes that are unlikely to upstage their clothing or face, while other women see their shoes as icebreakers or crowd-pleasers. One thing's for sure, a shoe should never have the kind of extroverted personality that causes it to stop the conversation when it walks into a room.

However, shoes shouldn't always be chosen as an afterthought to match an outfit. Sometimes you should start with the shoes, and then keep them in mind as the focal part of your look as you plan the rest of your outfit.

» Styles and occasions

There aren't many hard-and-fast rules when matching shoes to an outfit—it should be whatever you feel is an expression of your look. However, shoes do have the ability to make an outfit appear dressier or more casual, so bear in mind the occasion when selecting your shoes for an event. At the same time, certain styles and outfits marry better than others, and there are various classic combinations that are worth trying.

Flats: Ballets, pumps, lace-ups, clogs, or sandals are natural companions for narrow or cropped trousers and short or long skirts, but they don't fare well with mid-length skirts because they make legs appear disproportionately short.

Oxfords, loafers, or strappy stilettos: All of these look good with baggy trousers or tailored suits.

Stiletto heels: A dramatic heel works well with sleek clothing, such as a pencil skirt or tapered trousers.

Wedges: Wear these with bootcut jeans or flared trousers, sundresses, and slinky skirts.

Platforms: A platform shoe suits everything from cuffed shorts to day or evening dresses with flowing silhouettes.

Kitten heels: You can play up almost any outfit with kitten heels, from a cocktail dress to capri trousers.

Knee-length boots: Universally flatter most outfits, in particular, long or short skirts and jeans.

High-heeled sandals: Wear these to neutralize a formal or overtly feminine dress.

Mid-heeled mules: Add elegance to any number of casual outfits—trousers to dresses to suits—with a pair of mid-heeled mules. They look particularly sharp teamed with a suit that has a masculine cut.

Sneakers: These are in their element when worn with gym attire, yoga pants, sweatsuits, or jeans.

» **Office attire**

For everyday wear, the choice is really yours based on your individual taste—everyone will have their own opinion on what is appropriate for an occasion.

For work wear, however, there do tend to be guidelines to follow, particularly within offices where there are dress codes, and it is important to convey the right impression. In these cases conservative, medium-height wedges or pumps are a safe bet, as they are neutrally professional when worn with skirts. Boots or flats are suitable office mates for trousers. Super-high sandals or tall mules, over-the-knee boots, or extremely chunky soles are not generally thought of as work appropriate

» Color

The choice of shoe color is also very subjective and dependent on individual tastes. Black is still a staple that's acceptable with all types of clothing, no matter the style or season. The only real exception to that rule is pastel-colored evening wear, where a neutral hue trumps.

Otherwise, it is a matter of personal preference, and whether you like your footwear in colors that complement your outfit or that make a bold contrasting statement. Red shoes always make an impact and are rarely apropos in a professional scenario. Metallic colors rather than black or brown tend to elongate the foot. Bright colors work best on small feet while dark colors minimize the size of large feet.

Flattering styles

Certain styles of footwear are more flattering for different shapes and heights. It is best to experiment with what works well for your particular shape, and the effect will depend on the overall outfit, but there are some general guidelines to bear in mind.

>> **Boots**
Flattering boots don't uncover or cut off your leg at its thickest point which is why knee-high boots that end just as the leg tapers into the knee are universally flattering. Stretchy boots are kind to heavy ankles and they slim muscular calfs. High-heeled boots coordinated to the color of an outfit create a lengthening block of color that optically elongates the body.

>> **Toe shapes**
Short women should avoid ankle and T-straps as well as any decoration that interrupts the line of the leg. Opt instead for sandals that show more skin and feature tapered or pointed toes that optically extend the leg proportions. Weighty women are best to avoid rounded or oval toes, because pointed toes resolve their shape better. Round and square toes suit medium height to tall frames and long feet.

>> **High heels**
High heels are generally flattering but when they are above 4 inches they can actually make a short woman appear shorter, because they are proportionately overwhelming.

» **Flat shoes**
Most women can't pull off completely flat shoes and still look leggy. Ballet slippers have universal appeal for their comfort and convenience, but their delicacy foreshortens and adds optical heft to muscular legs.

» **Chunky shoes**
Women who carry volume in their torso can carry off chunky shoes, and wedges can help balance thicker ankles and calves.

» **Sandals**
Women with petite proportions should avoid gladiator sandals along with open shoes that feature ankle straps, cuffs, or ties.

» **Decorative details**
Bows, buckles, and lace overlays make feet appear more petite.

132

» Discover

Museums and exhibitions

Shoe museums provide intriguing collections of beautiful and curious shoes, and can provide a fascinating historical insight as well. Here are some of the most important ones around the world.

Bata Shoe Museum

327 Bloor Street West, Toronto, Ontario
M5S 1W7, Canada

Tel: 416 979 7799, www.batashoemuseum.ca

The Bata Shoe Museum houses a world-class collection of more than 12,000 artefacts spanning 4,500 years of history, and actively supports a mandate to research, exhibit, and publish on the cultural, historical, and sociological value of footwear. The museum has three temporary galleries as well as a large permanent gallery where exhibitions focused on all manner of footwear, from ancient to high fashion, are displayed.

Costume Institute at the Metropolitan Museum of Art

1000 Fifth Avenue, New York, NY 10028, USA

Tel: 212 535 7710, www.metmuseum.org

The Met houses the largest costume collection in the world, representing five continents and seven centuries, and periodically exhibits their incredibly vast shoe archive.

Marikina Shoe Museum

J.P. Rozal Street, Santa Elena, Marikina City,
Manila PH, 1800 Philippines

Tel: +63 2 646 1634

Founded in 2001 in the shoe capital of the Philippines, this museum displays footwear once worn by the country's former presidents and politicians. This includes the collection of Ferragamo, Givenchy, Christian Dior, and Chanel models once owned by one of the country's former dictators, Imelda Marcos (close to 750 pairs, all in size 8½).

Musee International de la Chaussure

2 rue Saint-Marie, 26100 Romans sue Isere,
France

Tel: +33 4 75 05 51 81

At the beginning of the 19th century, Romans had more than a dozen active tanneries and the region is regarded as the capital of the French footwear industry. This museum houses about 8,250 pairs of shoes spanning 4,000 years of history, with utilitarian and artistic highlights from the 20th and 21st centuries including the Charles Jourdan archive.

Museo del Calzado

Avenida de Chapi, 32, 03600 Elda, Alicante, Spain
Tel: +34 965 3830 21, www.museocalzado.com

This museum pays tribute to the Elda industrial region that primarily revolved around footwear. As well as footwear it houses machinery centered around the production of shoe lasts.

Northampton Museum and Art Gallery

Guildhall Road, Northampton, NN1 1DP, UK

Tel +44 (0)1604 838 111,
www.northampton.gov.us/museums

A gem of a shoe museum that's regarded as a national treasure. Rotating exhibitions may include an exquisite pair of 17th-century latchet tie shoes, a handful of 18th-century French heels, a grouping of stilettos, or even a platform once worn by a Spice Girl.

Salvatore Ferragamo Museum

Palazzo Spini Feroni at Piazza Santa Trinita 5/R, 50123 Florence, Italy

Tel: +39 055 3562846,
www.museoferragamo.it

Opened in 1995, this compact space contains four rooms filled with 13,000 of Ferragamo's original shoes, lasts, photographs, and 40 years of working documents plus a small collection of 18th- and 19th-century shoes.

Shoe Icons

Tel: +7 (499) 124 71 68, www.shoe-icons.com

A virtual shoe museum and extensive private collection of footwear that's housed in Moscow, it contains more than 1,500 pairs of shoes dating from the 17th century until the present day. It was founded in 2003 to produce exhibitions, publish books, calendars, and catalogs pertaining to

Words from the wise

Elizabeth Semmelhack, Senior
Curator of the Bata Shoe Museum

» Sticker shock

Designers such as Christian Louboutin have proven
that the soles of high heels can be quite eye-
catching. The flash of red revealed when a woman
walks in his shoes has made them some of the most
desirable items of fashion. Despite all of this new
attention on the soles of high-heeled shoes, many
fashionistas make the regrettable mistake of
forgetting to remove stickers from the soles of their
new shoes. This is a special hazard for shoes bought
on sale. Everyone loves a bargain, however,
advertising one's good fortune by forgetting to
remove the price tag is a fashion faux pas. The Bata
Shoe Museum's conservator, Ada Hopkins, advises
that stickers be gently pulled away from the sole and
any remaining adhesive be removed with an eraser.
Solvents or water should be avoided as they could
damage the shoes.

shoes, and to present footwear as more than just historical artifacts.

V&A South Kensington

Cromwell Road, London SW7 2RL, UK

Tel +44 (0)207 942 2000, www.vam.ac.uk

A fashion and textile collection dating from Egyptian times to the present day. It includes a wonderful collection of mid-19th-century children's shoes and 18th-century brocade shoes that are exhibited on occasion. The bookstore carries a well-edited range of shoe books.

Virtual Shoe Museum

www.virtualshoemuseum.com

Netherlands-based Liza Snook's passion for shoes developed into this social networking site for designers, shoe lovers, and curators. It's intended to be an inspirational showcase for new materials and in-process ideas, as well as a virtual exhibition space for displaying experimental shoe designs that teeter between art and function. Designers that are showcased include Kobi Levi from Israel, Egbert van der Does from Norway, Tetsuya Uenobe from Japan, and Rosanne Bergama from the Netherlands.

Further reading and resources

There are a number of online resources where you can find more information about the latest news and brand collections, from personal blogs to industry magazines and news sites.

Sea of Shoes

www.seaofshoes.com

Blogger Jane Aldridge started this blog in 2007 as a photo diary of her personally-styled ensembles and she has evolved into a fashion world insider.

Manolo's Shoe Blog

www.shoeblogs.com

Established in 2004, this blog is a verbal parody of Manolo Blahnik by an anonymous New Yorker who chats about shoes and celebrities in a quirky, witty, and slightly bizarre style. He/she has a cult following and is endorsed by the master designer himself.

Footwear News

www.footwearnews.com

A venerable trade newspaper covering the business side of the shoe industry. Subscription-based, it is affiliated with *Women's Wear Daily*, profiles designers and highlights retail using the voice of seasoned journalists.

Running with Heels

www.runningwithheels.com

An online magazine dedicated to women who love shoes, it provides daily updates on style news, celebrity fashion, runway reports, and more.

Shoe Lust

www.shoelust.us

A portfolio of high-quality images of shoes submitted by shoe companies, aficionados, and street photographers taken during the collections, reblogged, or appropriated from Flickr. The shots run with an attribution but no comments from readers or bloggers.

Shoewawa

www.shoewawa.com

The UK's first online "megazine" that's devoted to shoe shoppers. Owned by Aigua Media, it draws its editorial content from a mix of bloggers and fashion journalists and covers street fashion as well as runway shows. Fast paced with active reader comments, one of its most popular posts is the Ugly Shoe of the Week.

Glossary

Antiqued leather Double process of dyeing leather by layering a dark over light color to create a contrasting distressed or aged appearance.

Arch High, curved part of the sole of the foot, located between the ball and the heel as well as the reciprocal, padded, shoe part.

Back seam Vertical center seam located at the back of a shoe or boot.

Ball Padded part of the foot between the toes and arch that takes the weight of the body when the heel is raised.

Brannock device Simple instrument used to measure the length, width, and arc or girth of the foot to ensure an accurate shoe fit.

Brogue Perforated and pinked leather decoration on an Oxford shoe.

Chaussons Ballet or gymnastic slippers.

Collar Rim or top line of the shoe where the foot enters.

Cordwainer Another term for a shoemaker.

Counter Stiff piece of material placed at a shoe's heel between the lining and the upper to help retain its shape.

Cuissarde Over the knee boot.

Eyelet A hole created for threading a lace that's usually enforced with a metal grommet.

Footbed Interior sole of a shoe designed to hold the entire foot.

Footbinding Chinese tradition of permanently bandaging young girls' feet in order to prevent normal growth.

Girth Circumference of a shoe last or foot measured around the ball of the foot.

Golden lotus The ideal 3-inch foot length for women with bound feet.

Heel breast Forward-facing side of the heel.

Heel seat Part of the shoe directly below where the heel of the foot rests and where the sole and heel are joined.

Instep Arched center portion of the foot, particularly its upper surface, between the toes and ankle.

Last Three-dimensional form of the foot, generally carved from wood that stands in for the foot during the shoe-making process.

Lotus shoes Cone- or sheath-shaped, embroidered silk

shoes worn by women with bound feet.

Moccasin Shoe where the sole, sides, and back are constructed from a single piece of leather that's attached to a vamp with whip stitching.

Nap The raised or fuzzy surface on certain treated (napped) cloths.

Nappa Supple version of sheepskin leather.

Nubuck Lightweight, supple leather that's buffed to a suede-like appearance and used on a shoe's upper.

Opanke Moccasin construction where one piece of leather becomes the upper and the sole.

Piping Decorative narrow strip of leather or fabric that typically follows the seam of a shoe.

Quarter The side of the shoe between the heel and the vamp.

Quarter lining Leather or fabric that lines the rear part of the shoe.

Shaft Portion of the boot from the middle of the arch to the top of the boot.

Shank (arch support) Part of the shoe that runs between the heel and the outsole, and sits under the arch of the foot.

Spigot Thin metal shaft used to reinforce stiletto heels.

Tanning The process of making leather from animal hides.

Throat Main opening of a shoe, extending from the vamp to the ankle.

Tongue Leather or cloth insert used to cover an opening in the vamp throat of a shoe.

Top lift Bottom-most part of a shoe's heel that comes into contact with the ground.

Turned shoe Flexible single sole made from two pieces of leather that are attached and then turned inside out, or right side out, to hide the seam between the sole and the upper.

Upper From heel to toe, the parts of the shoe that cover the top of the foot not including the sole.

Vamp Shoe part covering the front of the foot from the instep to the toe.

Welt The material that joins the sole to the upper.

Winkle picker English term for shoes with sharp, pointed toes worn in the 1950s.

Index

143

144